Table of Contents

Table of Contents

Name: _Jessica Crothers 8/6/01_

Nouns

A **noun** names a person, place, thing or idea.
There are several types of nouns.

Examples:
   proper nouns: Joe, Jefferson Memorial
   common nouns: dog, town
   concrete nouns: book, stove
   abstract nouns: fear, devotion
   collective nouns: audience, flock

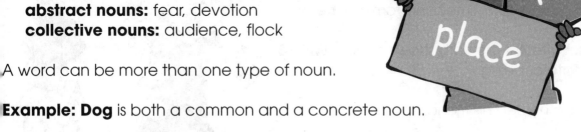

A word can be more than one type of noun.

Example: Dog is both a common and a concrete noun.

Directions: Write the type or types of each noun on the lines.

1. desk _noun   thing_
2. ocean _idea_
3. love _idea_
4. cat _common nouns_
5. herd _idea_
6. compassion _idea_
7. reputation _idea_
8. eyes _thing_
9. staff _person_
10. day _idea_
11. Roosevelt Building _place_
12. Mr. Timken _Person_
13. life _person_
14. porch _thing_
15. United States _Place_

Name: _Jessica Chromy 7/16/01_

Verbs

A **verb** is a word that tells what something does or that something exists.

There are two types of verbs: **action** and **state of being**.

Examples:
   Action: run, read
   State of being: feel, sound, taste, stay, look, appear, grow, seem, smell and forms of **be**

Directions: Write **A** if the verb shows action. Write **S** if it shows state of being.

1. __A__ He helped his friend.

2. __S__ They appear happy and content.

3. __S__ Jordi drives to school each day.

4. __S__ The snowfall closed schools everywhere.

5. __A__ The dog sniffed at its food.

6. __S__ The meat tastes funny.

7. __A__ Did you taste the ice cream?

8. __A__ The young boy smelled the flowers.

9. __S__ She looked depressed.

10. __S__ The coach announced the dates of the scrimmage.

11. __A__ The owner of the store stocks all types of soda.

12. __S__ He dribbled the ball down the court.

13. __A__ "Everything seems to be in order," said the train conductor.

Name: _Jessica Chern 8/6/01_

Nouns and Verbs

Some words can be used as both nouns and verbs.

Example:
   The **bait** on his hook was a worm.
   He couldn't **bait** his hook.

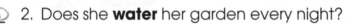

In the first sentence, **bait** is used as a **noun** because it names a thing. In the second sentence, **bait** is used as a **verb** because it shows action.

Directions: Write **noun** or **verb** for the word in bold in each sentence. The first one has been done for you.

verb   1. She **piloted** the small plane across the Pacific Ocean.

verb   2. Does she **water** her garden every night?

verb   3. Did you **rebel** against the rules?

bait   4. Dad will pound the fence **post** into the ground.

verb   5. That was good **thinking**!

verb   6. I **object** to your language!

verb   7. He planned to become a **pilot** after graduation.

bait   8. The teacher will **post** the new school calendar.

bait   9. She was **thinking** of a donut.

verb   10. The **object** of the search was forgotten.

verb   11. She was a **rebel** in high school.

bait   12. Would you like fresh **water** for your tea?

Simple Subjects

The **simple subject** of a sentence tells who or what the sentence is about. It is a noun or a pronoun.

Example: My **mom** is turning forty this year.
Mom is the simple subject.

Directions: Circle the simple subject in each sentence.

1. The (cat) ate all its food.

2. They watched the (basketball) game.

3. Loretta is going to lunch with (her friend).

4. José likes strawberry jam on (his) toast.

5. The (reporter) interviewed the victim.

6. (She) turned down the volume.

7. The farm (animals) waited to be fed.

8. Can (you) lift weights?

9. The (fan) did little to cool the hot room.

10. (Thomas Jefferson) was one of the founding fathers of our country.

11. (I) have a lot to do tonight.

12. Will (you) go to the movie with us?

13. (We) enjoyed the day at the park.

14. (Our) (pet) is a (dog).

15. (She) retrieved (her) homework from the garbage.

Personal Pronouns

Personal pronouns take the place of nouns. They refer to people or things. **I, me, we, she, he, him, her, you, they, them, us** and **it** are personal pronouns.

Directions: Circle the personal pronouns in each sentence.

1. He is a terrific friend.

2. Would you open the door?

3. Jim and I will arrive at ten o'clock.

4. Can you pick me up at the mall after dinner?

5. What did you do yesterday?

6. They are watching the game on television.

7. Jessie's mom took us to the movies.

8. She writes novels.

9. They gave us the refrigerator.

10. Is this the answer she intended to give?

11. What is it?

12. The dog yelped when it saw the cat.

13. I admire him.

14. We parked the bikes by the tree.

15. The ants kept us from enjoying our picnic.

16. James gives his dog a bath once a week.

Possessive Pronouns

Possessive pronouns show ownership. **My, mine, your, yours, his, her, hers, their, theirs, our, ours** and **its** are possessive pronouns.

Directions: Circle the possessive pronouns in each sentence.

1. My dogs chase cats continually.

2. Jodi put her sunglasses on the dashboard.

3. His mother and mine are the same age.

4. The cat licked its paw.

5. Their anniversary is February 1.

6. This necklace is yours.

7. We will carry our luggage into the airport.

8. Our parents took us to dinner.

9. My brother broke his leg.

10. Her report card was excellent.

11. Raspberry jam is my favorite.

12. Watch your step!

13. The house on the left is mine.

14. My phone number is unlisted.

15. Our garden is growing out of control.

16. Our pumpkins are ten times larger than theirs.

Name: _Jessica Chem_ 7/19/01

Interrogative Pronouns

An **interrogative pronoun** asks a question. There are three interrogative pronouns: **who, what** and **which**.

Use **who** when speaking of persons.
Use **what** when speaking of things.
Use **which** when speaking of persons or things.

Examples:
    Who will go? **What** will you do? **Which** of these is yours?

Who becomes **whom** when it is a direct object or an object of a preposition. The possessive form of **whom** is **whose**.

Examples:
    To **whom** will you write?
    Whose computer is that?

Directions: Write the correct interrogative pronoun.

1. ___What___ wet raincoat is this?

2. ___Who___ is the president of the United States?

3. ___What___ is your name?

4. ___Who___ dog made this muddy mess?

5. ___Which___ cat ran away?

6. ___Which___ of you is the culprit?

7. ___What___ was your grade on the last test?

8. To ___who___ did you report?

9. ___What___ do you believe now?

10. ___Who___ is the leader of this English study group?

Name: _Jessica Cheem 7/19/05_

Personal and Possessive Pronouns

Directions: Write personal or possessive pronouns in the blanks to take the place of the words in bold. The first one has been done for you.

__They   him__   1. **Maisie and Marni** told **Trent** they would see him later.

~~Them~~ He him   2. **Spencer** told **Narcee and Sandi** good-bye.

It is   3. **The bike** was parked near **Aaron's** house.

They   4. **Maria, Matt and Greg** claimed the car was new.

~~Theress~~ Theirs   5. The dishes were **the property of Cindy and Jake**.

Hers   6. Is this **Carole's**?

Hear Theres   7. **Jon** walked near **Jessica and Esau's** house.

It   8. **The dog** barked all night long!

She Hear   9. **Dawn** fell and hurt **Dawn's** knee.

They It's   10. **Cory and Devan** gave the dog **the dog's** dinner.

We them   11. **Tori and I** gave **Brett and Reggie** a ride home.

They   12. Do **Josh and Andrea** like cats?

They us   13. **Sasha and Keesha** gave **Josh and me** a ride home.

hears   14. Is this sweater **Marni's**?

It   15. The cat meowed because **the cat** was hungry.

Name: _Jessica Cherm 7/19/01_

Pronoun/Antecedent Agreement

Often, a **pronoun** is used in place of a noun to avoid repeating the noun again in the same sentence. The noun that a pronoun refers to is called its **antecedent**. The word "antecedent" means "going before."

If the noun is singular, the pronoun that takes its place must also be singular. If the noun is plural, the pronoun that takes its place must also be plural. This is called *agreement* between the pronoun and its antecedent.

Examples:
   Mary (singular noun) said **she** (singular pronoun) would dance.
   The **dogs** (plural noun) took **their** (plural pronoun) dishes outside.

When the noun is singular and the gender unknown, it is correct to use either "his" or "his or her."

Directions: Rewrite the sentences so the pronouns and nouns agree. The first one has been done for you.

1. Every student opened their book.

   Every student opened his book.

   Also correct: **Every student opened his or her book.**

2. Has anyone lost their wallet lately?

   Has anyone found his or hers wallet ~~yet~~ yet.

3. Somebody found the wallet under their desk.

   Did anyone found any wallet under his or hers desk.

4. Someone will have to file their report.

   Someone will have to file their report.

5. Every dog has their day!

   Every dog has their own day

6. I felt Ted had mine best interests at heart.

   I felt Ted had ~~mine~~ my e best interests at heart

Name: _Jessica Chen_ 7/19/01

Pronoun/Antecedent Agreement

Directions: Write a pronoun that agrees with the antecedent.

1. Donald said ___us___ would go to the store.

2. My friend discovered ___the___ wallet had been stolen.

3. The cat licked ___his___ paw.

4. Did any woman here lose ~~there~~ thier necklace?

5. Someone will have to give ___their___ report.

6. Jennifer wished ___that___ had not come.

7. All the children decided ___that___ would attend.

8. My grandmother hurt ___her___ back while gardening.

9. Jerry, Marco and I hope ___that___ win the game.

10. Sandra looked for ___her___ missing homework.

11. The family had ___many___ celebration.

12. My dog jumps out of ___the___ pen.

13. Somebody needs to remove ___her___ clothes from this chair.

14. Everything has ___a___ place in Grandma's house.

15. The team will receive ___thier___ uniforms on Monday.

16. Each artist wants ___to___ painting to win the prize.

12

Name: _____

Appositives

An **appositive** is a noun or pronoun placed after another noun or pronoun to further identify or rename it. An appositive and the words that go with it are usually set off from the rest of the sentence with commas. Commas are not used if the appositive tells "which one."

Example: Angela's mother, **Ms. Glover**, will visit our school.

Commas are needed because **Ms. Glover** renames Angela's mother.

Example: Angela's neighbor Joan will visit our school.

Commas are not needed because the appositive "Joan" tells **which** neighbor.

Directions: Write the appositive in each sentence in the blank. The first one has been done for you.

__Tina__   1. My friend Tina wants a horse.

_____   2. She subscribes to the magazine *Horses*.

_____   3. Her horse is the gelding "Brownie."

_____   4. We rode in her new car, a convertible.

_____   5. Her gift was jewelry, a bracelet.

_____   6. Have you met Ms. Abbott, the senator?

_____   7. My cousin Karl is very shy.

_____   8. Do you eat the cereal Oaties?

_____   9. Kiki's cat, Samantha, will eat only tuna.

_____ 10. My last name, Jones, is very common.

Name: *Jessica Chem 7/8/01*

Verb Tense

Tense is the way a verb is used to express time. To explain what is happening right now, use the **present tense**.

Example: He **is singing** well. He **sings** well.

To explain what has already happened, use the **past tense**.

Example: He **sang** well.

To explain what will happen, use the **future tense**.

Example: He **will sing** well.

Directions: Rewrite each sentence so the verbs are in the same tense. The first one has been done for you.

1. He ran, he jumped, then he is flying.

   <u>He ran, he jumped, then he flew.</u>

2. He was crying, then he will stop.

   He was crying, the he will stop

3. She feels happy, but she was not sure why.

   She feels happy, but she was not, sure why

4. He is my friend, so was she.

   He is my friend, so was she

5. She bit into the cake and says it is good.

   She bit into the cake and says it is good

6. He laughs first and then told us the joke.

   He laughts first and then told us the joke.

Verb Tense

Directions: Write a sentence using the present tense of each verb.

1. walk _____

_____

2. dream _____

_____

3. achieve _____

_____

Directions: Write a sentence using the past tense of each verb.

4. dance _____

_____

5. study _____

_____

6. hike _____

_____

Directions: Write a sentence using the future tense of each verb.

7. bake _____

_____

8. write _____

_____

9. talk _____

_____

Verb Tense

Verbs can be **present**, **past** or **past participle**.

Add **d** or **ed** to form the past tense.

Past-participle verbs also use a helping verb such as **has** or **have**.

Examples:

Present	Past	Past Participle
help	helped	has or have helped
skip	skipped	has or have skipped

Directions: Write the past and past-participle forms of each present tense verb.

Present	Past	Past Participle
1. paint	painted	has (have) painted
2. dream		
3. play		
4. approach		
5. hop		
6. climb		
7. dance		
8. appear		
9. watch		
10. dive		
11. hurry		
12. discover		
13. decorate		
14. close		
15. jump		

Irregular Verb Forms

The past tense of most verbs is formed by adding **ed**. Verbs that do not follow this format are called **irregular verbs**.

The irregular verb chart shows a few of the many verbs with irregular forms.

Irregular Verb Chart		
Present Tense	**Past Tense**	**Past Participle**
go	went	has, have or had gone
do	did	has, have or had done
fly	flew	has, have or had flown
grow	grew	has, have or had grown
ride	rode	has, have or had ridden
see	saw	has, have or had seen
sing	sang	has, have or had sung
swim	swam	has, have or had swum
throw	threw	has, have or had thrown

The words **have** and **has** can be separated from the irregular verb by other words in the sentence.

Directions: Choose the correct verb form from the chart to complete the sentences. The first one has been done for you.

1. The pilot had never before ___**flown**___ that type of plane.

2. She put on her bathing suit and _____ 2 miles.

3. The tall boy had _____ 2 inches over the summer.

4. She insisted she had _____ her homework.

5. He _____ them walking down the street.

6. She _____ the horse around the track.

7. The pitcher has _____ the ball many times.

8. He can _____ safely in the deepest water.

Irregular Verb Forms

Directions: Use the irregular verb chart on the previous page. Write the correct verb form to complete each sentence.

1. Has she ever _____ carrots in her garden?

2. She was so angry she _____ a tantrum.

3. The bird had sometimes _____ from its cage.

4. The cowboy has never _____ that horse before.

5. Will you _____ to the store with me?

6. He said he had often _____ her walking on his street.

7. She insisted she has not _____ taller this year.

8. He _____ briskly across the pool.

9. Have the insects _____ away?

10. Has anyone _____ my sister lately?

11. He hasn't _____ the dishes once this week!

12. Has she been _____ out of the game for cheating?

13. I haven't _____ her yet today.

14. The airplane _____ slowly by the airport.

15. Have you _____ your bike yet this week?

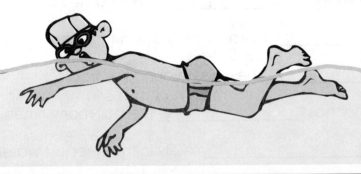

Name:_____

Simple Predicates

The **simple predicate** of a sentence tells what the subject does, is doing, did or will do. The simple predicate is always a verb.

Example:
My mom **is turning** forty this year.
"Is turning" is the simple predicate.

Directions: Underline the simple predicate in each sentence. Include all helping verbs.

1. I bought school supplies at the mall.

2. The tiger chased its prey.

3. Mark will be arriving shortly.

4. The hamburgers are cooking now.

5. We will attend my sister's wedding.

6. The dental hygienist cleaned my teeth.

7. My socks are hanging on the clothesline.

8. Where are you going?

9. The dog is running toward its owner.

10. Ramos watched the tornado in fear.

11. Please wash the dishes after dinner.

12. My dad cleaned the garage yesterday.

13. We are going hiking at Yellowstone today.

14. The picture shows our entire family at the family picnic.

15. Our coach will give us a pep talk before the game.

© 1999 American Education Publishing Co.

Parallel Structure

Parts of a sentence are **parallel** when they "match" grammatically and structurally.

Faulty parallelism occurs when the parts of a sentence do not match grammatically and structurally.

For sentences to be parallel, all parts of a sentence—including the verbs, nouns and phrases—must match. This means that, in most cases, verbs should be in the same tense.

Examples:
 Correct: She liked running, jumping and swinging outdoors.
 Incorrect: She liked running, jumping and to swing outdoors.

In the correct sentence, all three of the actions the girl liked to do end in **ing**. In the incorrect sentence, they do not.

Directions: Rewrite the sentences so all elements are parallel. The first one has been done for you.

1. Politicians like making speeches and also to shake hands.

 Politicians like making speeches and shaking hands.

2. He liked singing, acting and to perform in general.

 He liked singing, acting, perform in general.

3. The cake had icing, sprinkles and also has small candy hearts.

 The cake had icing sprinkles and also has small candy hearts.

4. The drink was cold, frosty and also is a thirst-quencher.

 The drink was cold, frosty and also is a thirst-quenchers.

5. She was asking when we would arrive, and I told her.

 She was asking when we would arrive, and I told her.

6. Liz felt like shouting, singing and to jump.

 Liz felt like shouting singin and to jump.

Subject/Verb Agreement

Singular subjects require singular verbs. **Plural subjects** require plural verbs. The subject and verb must agree in a sentence.

Example:
    Singular: My dog runs across the field.
    Plural: My dogs run across the field.

Directions: Circle the correct verb in each sentence.

1. Maria (talk/talks) to me each day at lunch.

2. Mom, Dad and I (is/are) going to the park to play catch.

3. Mr. and Mrs. Ramirez (dance/dances) well together.

4. Astronauts (hope/hopes) for a successful shuttle mission.

5. Trees (prevent/prevents) erosion.

6. The student (is/are) late.

7. She (ask/asks) for directions to the senior high gym.

8. The elephants (plod/plods) across the grassland to the watering hole.

9. My friend's name (is/are) Rebecca.

10. Many people (enjoy/enjoys) orchestra concerts.

11. The pencils (is/are) sharpened.

12. My backpack (hold/holds) a lot of things.

13. The wind (blow/blows) to the south.

14. Sam (collect/collects) butterflies.

15. They (love/loves) cotton candy.

Dangling Modifiers

A **dangling modifier** is a word or group of words that does not modify what it is supposed to modify. To correct dangling modifiers, supply the missing words to which the modifiers refer.

Examples:
   Incorrect: While doing the laundry, the dog barked.
   Correct: While I was doing the laundry, the dog barked.

In the **incorrect** sentence, it sounds as though the dog is doing the laundry. In the **correct** sentence, it's clear that **I** is the subject of the sentence.

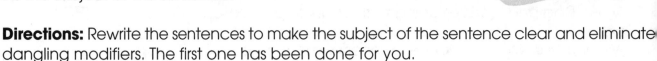

Directions: Rewrite the sentences to make the subject of the sentence clear and eliminate dangling modifiers. The first one has been done for you.

1. While eating our hot dogs, the doctor called.

While we were eating our hot dogs, the doctor called.

2. Living in Cincinnati, the ball park is nearby.

   Living in Cincinnati, the ball park is nearby

3. While watching the movie, the TV screen went blank.

   While watching the movie, the TV screen went blanks

4. While listening to the concert, the lights went out.

   While listening to the concert, the lights went out

5. Tossed regularly, anyone can make great salad.

   Tossed regularly, anyone can make great salad

6. The programmer saw something on his screen that surprised him.

   The programmer saw something on his screen that surprised
   him.

Name: _Jessica Chern #15 7/16/01_

Review

Directions: Rewrite the sentences to correct the faulty parallels.

1. The cookies were sweet, crunchy and are delicious.

   The cookies were sweet, crunchy and are delicious.

2. The town was barren, windswept and is empty.

   The town was barren windswept and is empty.

3. The dog was black, long-haired and is quite friendly.

   The dog was black, long-haired and is quite friendly

4. My favorite dinners are macaroni and cheese, spaghetti and I loved fish.

   My favorite dinners are macaroni and cheese, spaghetti and loved fish.

Directions: Rewrite the sentences to make the verb tenses consistent.

5. We laughed, cried and were jumping for joy.

   We laughed, cried and were jumping for joy.

6. She sang, danced and was doing somersaults.

   She sang, danced and was doing somersaults.

7. The class researched, studied and were writing their reports.

   The class researched studied and were writing their report

8. Bob and Sue talked about their vacation and share their experiences.

   Bob and Sue talked about their vaction and share their experience

Directions: Circle the pronouns that agree with their antecedents.

9. She left (her/their) purse at the dance.

10. Each dog wagged (its/their) tail.

11. We walked to (our/he) car.

12. The lion watched (his/its) prey.

23

Name: _____

Review

Directions: Rewrite the sentences to correct the dangling modifiers.

1. Living nearby, the office was convenient for her.

   _____

2. While doing my homework, the doorbell rang.

   _____

3. Watching over her shoulder, she hurried away.

   _____

4. Drinking from the large mug, he choked.

   _____

Directions: Circle the correct pronouns.

5. She laughed at my brother and (I/me).

6. At dawn, (he and I/him and me) were still talking.

7. Someone left (his or her/their) coat on the floor.

8. Lauren said (her/she) would not be late.

Directions: Circle the appositive.

9. The school nurse, Ms. Franklin, was worried about him.

10. The car, a Volkswagen, was illegally parked.

11. My hero, Babe Ruth, was an outstanding baseball player.

12. Is that car, the plum-colored one, for sale?

13. Will Mr. Zimmer, Todd's father, buy that car?

Name:_____

Adjectives

Adjectives describe nouns.

Examples:
 tall girl
 soft voice
 clean hands

Directions: Circle the adjectives. Underline the nouns they describe. Some sentences may have more than one set of adjectives and nouns.

1. The lonely man sat in the dilapidated house.

2. I hope the large crop of grapes will soon ripen.

3. The white boxes house honeybees.

4. My rambunctious puppy knocked over the valuable flower vase.

5. The "unsinkable" *Titanic* sank after striking a gigantic iceberg.

6. His grades showed his tremendous effort.

7. There are many purple flowers in the large arrangement.

8. These sweet peaches are the best I've tasted.

9. The newsletter describes several educational workshops.

10. The rodeo featured professional riders and funny clowns.

11. My evening pottery class is full of very interesting people.

12. My older brother loves his new pickup truck.

13. Tami's family bought a big-screen TV.

Name:_____

Adverbs

Adverbs tell when, where or how an action occurred.

Examples:
   I'll go **tomorrow**. (when)
   I sleep **upstairs**. (where)
   I screamed **loudly**. (how)

Directions: Circle the adverb and underline the verb it modifies. Write the question (when, where or how) the adverb answers.

1. I ran quickly toward the finish line. _____

2. Today, we will receive our report cards. _____

3. He swam smoothly through the pool. _____

4. Many explorers searched endlessly for
   new lands. _____

5. He looked up into the sky. _____

6. My friend drove away in her new car. _____

7. Later, we will search for your missing wallet. _____

8. Most kings rule their kingdoms regally. _____

9. New plants must be watered daily. _____

10. The stream near our house is heavily polluted. _____

11. My brother likes to dive backward into
    our pool. _____

Name: _____

Adjectives and Adverbs

Directions: Write **adjective** or **adverb** in the blanks to describe the words in bold. The first one has been done for you.

adjective   1. Her **old** boots were caked with mud.

_____ 2. The baby was **cranky**.

_____ 3. He took the test **yesterday**.

_____ 4. I heard the **funniest** story last week!

_____ 5. She left her wet shoes **outside**.

_____ 6. Isn't that the **fluffiest** cat you've ever seen?

_____ 7. He ran **around** the track twice.

_____ 8. Our elderly neighbor lady seems **lonely**.

_____ 9. His **kind** smile lifted my dragging spirits.

_____ 10. **Someday** I'll meet the friend of my dreams!

_____ 11. His cat never meows **indoors**.

_____ 12. Carlos hung his new shirts **back** in the closet.

_____ 13. Put that valuable vase **down** immediately!

_____ 14. She is the most **joyful** child!

_____ 15. Jonathan's wool sweater is totally **moth-eaten**.

Adjectives: Positive, Comparative and Superlative

There are three degrees of comparison adjectives: **positive**, **comparative** and **superlative**. The **positive degree** is the adjective itself. The **comparative** and **superlative** degrees are formed by adding **er** and **est**, respectively, to most one-syllable adjectives. The form of the word changes when the adjective is irregular, for example, **good**, **better**, **best**.

Most adjectives of two or more syllables require the words "more" or "most" to form the comparative and superlative degrees.

Examples:

Positive:	big	eager
Comparative:	bigger	more eager
Superlative:	biggest	most eager

Directions: Write the positive, comparative or superlative forms of these adjectives.

	Positive	Comparative	Superlative
1.	hard	_____	_____
2.	_____	happier	_____
3.	_____	_____	most difficult
4.	cold	_____	_____
5.	_____	easier	_____
6.	_____	_____	largest
7.	little	_____	_____
8.	_____	shinier	_____
9.	round	_____	_____
10.	_____	_____	most beautiful

Adverbs: Positive, Comparative and Superlative

here are also three degrees of comparison adverbs: **positive**, **comparative** and **uperlative**. They follow the same rules as adjectives.

xample:

Positive:	rapidly	far	
Comparative:	more rapidly	farther	
Superlative:	most rapidly	farthest	

irections: Write the positive, comparative or superlative forms of these adverbs.

Positive	Comparative	Superlative
1. easily	_____	_____
2. _____	more quickly	_____
3. _____	_____	most hopefully
4. bravely	_____	_____
5. _____	more strongly	_____
6. near	_____	_____
7. _____	_____	most cleverly
8. _____	more gracefully	_____
9. _____	_____	most humbly
0. excitedly	_____	_____
1. _____	more handsomely	_____
2. slowly	_____	_____

Prepositions

A **preposition** is a word that comes before a noun or pronoun and shows the relationship of that noun or pronoun to some other word in the sentence.

The **object of a preposition** is the noun or pronoun that follows a preposition and adds to its meaning.

A **prepositional phrase** includes the preposition, the object of the preposition and all modifiers.

Example:
She gave him a pat **on his back**.
On is the preposition.
Back is the object of the preposition.
His is a possessive pronoun.

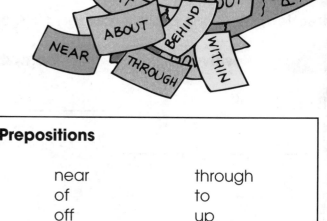

Common Prepositions			
about	down	near	through
above	for	of	to
across	from	off	up
at	in	on	with
behind	into	out	within
by	like	past	without

Directions: Underline the prepositional phrases. Circle the prepositions. Some sentences have more than one prepositional phrase. The first one has been done for you.

1. He claimed he felt (at) home only (on) the West Coast.

2. She went up the street, then down the block.

3. The famous poet was near death.

4. The beautiful birthday card was from her father.

5. He left his wallet at home.

6. Her speech was totally without humor and boring as well.

7. I think he's from New York City.

8. Kari wanted to go with her mother to the mall.

Prepositions

irections: Complete the sentences by writing objects
or the prepositions. The first one has been done for you.

1. He was standing at **the corner of Fifth and Main.** _____

2. She saw her friend across _____

3. Have you ever looked beyond _____

4. His contact lens fell into _____

5. Have you ever gone outside without _____

6. She was anxious for _____

7. Is that dog from _____

8. She was daydreaming and walked past _____

9. The book was hidden behind _____

10. The young couple had fallen in _____

11. She insisted she was through _____

12. He sat down near _____

13. She forgot her umbrella at _____

14. Have you ever thought of _____

15. Henry found his glasses on _____

Object of a Preposition

The **object of a preposition** is the noun or pronoun that follows the preposition and add
to its meaning.

Example:
   Correct: Devan smiled **at** (preposition) **Tori** (noun: object of the preposition) and **m**
      (pronoun: object of the same preposition.)
   Correct: Devan smiled at Tori. Devan smiled at me. Devan smiled at Tori and me.
   Incorrect: Devan smiled at Tori and I.

Tip: If you are unsure of the correct pronoun to use, pair each pronoun with the verb an
say the phrase out loud to find out which pronoun is correct.

Directions: Write the correct pronouns on the blanks. The first one has been done for you

him _____ 1. It sounded like a good idea to Sue and (he/him).

_____ 2. I asked Abby if I could attend with (her/she).

_____ 3. To (we/us), holidays are very important.

_____ 4. Between (we/us), we finished the job quickly.

_____ 5. They gave the award to (he and I/him and me).

_____ 6. The party was for my brother and (I/me).

_____ 7. I studied at (his/him) house.

_____ 8. Tanya and the others arrived late in spite of (they/their) fast car.

_____ 9. After (we/us) went to the zoo, we stopped at the museum.

_____ 10. The chips are in the bag on top of (his/him) refrigerator.

Name:_____

Direct Objects

A **direct object** is a noun or pronoun. It answers the question **who** or **what** after a verb.

Examples:
My mom baked **bread**.
Bread is the direct object. It tells **what** Mom baked.
We saw **Steve**.
Steve is the direct object. It tells **who** we saw.

Directions: Write a direct object in each sentence.

1. My dog likes _____. WHAT?

2. My favorite drink is _____. WHAT?

3. I saw _____ today. WHOM?

4. The car struck a _____. WHAT?

5. The fan blew _____ through the room. WHAT?

6. I packed a _____ for lunch. WHAT?

7. We watched _____ play basketball. WHOM?

8. I finished my _____. WHAT?

9. The artist sketched the _____. WHAT?

10. He greets _____ at the door. WHOM?

11. The team attended the victory _____. WHAT?

12. The beautician cut my _____. WHAT?

13. Tamika will write _____. WHAT?

Indirect Objects

An **indirect object** is a noun or pronoun which tells **to whom or what** or **for whom or what** the action is performed. An indirect object usually is found between a verb and a direct object.

Example:
    I gave **Ellen** my address.
    Ellen is the indirect object. It tells **to whom** I gave my address.

Directions: Circle the indirect objects. Underline the direct objects.

1. Joann told Mary the secret.

2. Advertisers promise consumers the world.

3. The dogs showed me their tricks.

4. Aunt Martha gave Rhonda a necklace for her birthday.

5. Ramon brought Mom a bouquet of fresh flowers.

6. I sent my niece a package for Christmas.

7. Mr. Dunbar left his wife a note before leaving.

8. Grandma and Grandpa made their friends dinner.

9. The baby handed her mom a toy.

10. Monica told Stephanie the recipe for meatloaf.

11. We sent Grandma a card.

12. The waiter served us dessert.

13. Mom and Dad sold us the farm.

Name: _____

Complete Sentences

A **complete sentence** has both a simple subject and a simple predicate. It is a complete thought. Sentences which are not complete are called **fragments**.

Example:
    Complete sentence: The wolf howled at the moon.
    Sentence fragment: Howled at the moon.

Directions: Write **C** on the line if the sentence is complete. Write **F** if it is a fragment.

1. _____ The machine is running.

2. _____ What will we do today?

3. _____ Knowing what I do.

4. _____ That statement is true.

5. _____ My parents drove to town.

6. _____ Watching television all afternoon.

7. _____ The storm devastated the town.

8. _____ Our friends can go with us.

9. _____ The palm trees bent in the wind.

10. _____ Spraying the fire all night.

Directions: Rewrite the sentence fragments from above to make them complete sentences.

_____

_____

_____

_____

_____

_____

Name:_____

Run-On Sentences

A **run-on sentence** occurs when two or more sentences are joined together without punctuation or a joining word. Run-on sentences should be divided into two or more separate sentences.

Example:
   Run-on sentence: My parents, sister, brother and I went to the park we saw many animals we had fun.
   Correct: My parents, sister, brother and I went to the park. We saw many animals and had fun.

Directions: Rewrite the run-on sentences correctly.

1. The dog energetically chased the ball I kept throwing him the ball for a half hour.

_____

_____

_____

2. The restaurant served scrambled eggs and bacon for breakfast I had some and they were delicious.

_____

_____

_____

3. The lightning struck close to our house it scared my little brother and my grandmother called to see if we were safe.

_____

_____

_____

_____

_____

Conjunctions

Conjunctions are joining words that connect two or more words or groups of words. The words **and**, **but**, **or**, **nor**, **so** and **because** are conjunctions.

Join two sentences with **and** when they are more or less equal.

Example: John will be there, **and** he will bring the punch.

Join two sentences with **but** when the second sentence contradicts the first.

Example: John will be there, **but** his brother will not.

Join two sentences with **or** or **nor** when they name a choice.

Example: John may bring punch, **or** he may bring soda.

Join two sentences with **because** or **so** when the second one names a reason for the first one.

Example: John will bring punch **because** he's on the refreshment committee.

Directions: Finish each sentence using the conjunction correctly. The first one has been done for you.

1. My best friend was absent, so _I ate lunch alone._ _____

2. The test was easy, but _____

3. I wanted to go because _____

4. We did our homework, and _____

5. We can go skating, or _____

6. I felt sick, so _____

7. Josh was sad because _____

8. We worked quickly, and _____

Conjunctions

The conjunctions **and**, **or**, **but** and **nor** can be used to make a compound subject, a compound predicate or a compound sentence.

Examples:
  Compound subject: My friend **and** I will go to the mall.
  Compound predicate: We ran **and** jumped in gym class.
  Compound sentence: I am a talented violinist,
                          but my father is better.

Directions: Write two sentences of your own in each section.

Compound subject:

1. _____

   _____

2. _____

   _____

Compound predicate:

1. _____

   _____

2. _____

   _____

Compound sentence:

1. _____

   _____

2. _____

   _____

Name:_____

Review

Directions: Write the missing verb tenses.

	Present	Past	Past Participle
1.	catch	_____	_____
2.	_____	stirred	_____
3.	_____	_____	has (have) baked
4.	go	_____	_____
5.	_____	said	_____

Directions: Circle the simple subject and underline the simple predicate in each sentence.

6. Maria got sunburned at the beach.

7. The class watched the program.

8. The tomatoes are ripening.

9. We went grocery shopping.

10. The cross country team practiced all summer.

Directions: Write the missing adjective or adverb forms below.

	Positive	Comparative	Superlative
11.	_____	more friendly	_____
12.	small	_____	_____
13.	_____	_____	most fun
14.	_____	more attractive	_____

Name: _____

Review

Directions: Circle the indirect objects. Underline the direct objects.

1. She gave her mom a television.

2. Mary bought Gloria a shirt.

3. The teacher gave Sid his report card.

4. He passed his sister the spaghetti.

5. Maya told Art the story.

Directions: Write a sentence for each part of speech.

6. Personal pronoun _____

_____

7. Possessive pronoun _____

_____

8. Interrogative pronoun _____

_____

9. Prepositional phrase _____

_____

10. Adjective in superlative form _____

_____

11. Adverb in comparative form _____

_____

12. Verb in past participle form _____

_____

Review

Directions: Write **noun** or **verb** to describe the words in bold.

_____ 1. She is one of the fastest **runners** I've seen.

_____ 2. She is **running** very fast!

_____ 3. She **thought** he was handsome.

_____ 4. Please share your **thoughts** with me.

_____ 5. I will **watch** the volleyball game on video.

_____ 6. The sailor fell asleep during his **watch**.

_____ 7. My grandmother believes my purchase was a real **find**.

_____ 8. I hope to **find** my lost books.

Directions: Rewrite the verb in the correct tense.

_____ 9. She **swim** across the lake in 2 hours.

_____ 10. He has **ride** horses for years.

_____ 11. Have you **saw** my sister?

_____ 12. She **fly** on an airplane last week.

_____ 13. My father had **instruct** me in the language.

_____ 14. I **drive** to the store yesterday.

_____ 15. The movie **begin** late.

_____ 16. Where **do** you go yesterday?

Directions: Circle the pronouns.

17. She and I told them to forget it!

18. They all wondered if her dad would drive his new car.

19. We want our parents to believe us.

20. My picture was taken at her home.

© 1999 American Education Publishing Co.

Review

Directions: Write **adjective** or **adverb** to describe the words in bold.

_____ 1. My **old** boyfriend lives nearby.

_____ 2. My old boyfriend lives **nearby**.

_____ 3. His hair looked **horrible**.

_____ 4. Have you heard this **silly** joke?

_____ 5. **Suddenly**, the door opened.

_____ 6. The **magnificent** lion raised its head.

_____ 7. I accomplished the task **yesterday**.

_____ 8. This party has **delicious** food.

Directions: Circle the prepositions.

9. He went in the door and up the stairs.

10. Is this lovely gift from you?

11. I was all for it, but the decision was beyond my power.

12. His speech dragged on into the night.

13. My great-grandmother's crystal dish is in the curio cabinet.

14. He received a trophy for his accomplishments on the team.

15. The President of the United States is on vacation.

16. Joel wrote an excellent essay about Christopher Columbus.

Name: _____

Commas

Use **commas** . . .

  . . . after introductory phrases

  . . . to set off nouns of direct address

  . . . to set off appositives from the words that go with them

  . . . to set off words that interrupt the flow of the sentence

  . . . to separate words or groups of words in a series

Examples:

Introductory phrase: Of course, I'd be happy to attend.

Noun of direct address: Ms. Williams, please sit here.

To set off appositives: Lee, **the club president**, sat beside me.

Words interrupting flow: My cousin, **who's 13**, will also be there.

Words in a series: I ate **popcorn, peanuts, oats** and **barley**.

    or   I ate **popcorn, peanuts, oats,** and **barley**.

Note: The final comma is optional when punctuating words in a series.

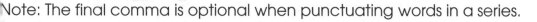

Directions: Identify how the commas are used in each sentence.

    Write: **I** for introductory phrase

          N for noun of direct address

          A for appositive

          WF for words interrupting flow

          WS for words in a series

_____ 1. Yes, she is my sister.

_____ 2. My teacher, Mr. Hopkins, is very fair.

_____ 3. Her favorite fruits are oranges, plums and grapes.

_____ 4. The city mayor, Carla Ellison, is quite young.

_____ 5. I will buy bread, milk, fruit and ice cream.

_____ 6. Her crying, which was quite loud, soon gave me a headache.

_____ 7. Stephanie, please answer the question.

_____ 8. So, do you know her?

_____ 9. Unfortunately, the item is not returnable.

_____ 10. My sister, my cousin and my friend will accompany me on vacation.

_____ 11. My grandparents, Rose and Bill, are both 57 years old.

43

Commas

Directions: Use commas to punctuate these sentences correctly.

Commas are important, and you should know when to use them!

COMMAS

1. I'll visit her however not until I'm ready.

2. She ordered coats gloves and a hat from the catalog.

3. Eun-Jung the new girl looked ill at ease.

4. Certainly I'll show Eun-Jung around school.

5. Yes I'll be glad to help her.

6. I paid nevertheless I was unhappy with the price.

7. I bought stamps envelopes and plenty of postcards.

8. No I told you I was not going.

9. The date November 12 was not convenient.

10. Her earache which kept her up all night stopped at dawn.

11. My nephew who loves bike riding will go with us.

12. He'll bring hiking boots a tent and food.

13. The cat a Himalayan was beautiful.

14. The tennis player a professional in every sense signed autographs.

15. No you can't stay out past 10:00 P.M.

Name:_____

Semicolons

A **semicolon** (;) signals a reader to pause longer than for a comma, but not as long as for a period. Semicolons are used between closely related independent clauses not joined by **and, or, nor, for, yet** or **but**.

An **independent clause** contains a complete idea and can stand alone.

Example: Rena was outgoing; her sister was shy.

Directions: Use semicolons to punctuate these sentences correctly. Some sentences require more than one semicolon.

1. Jeff wanted coffee Sally wanted milk.

2. I thought he was kind she thought he was grouchy.

3. "I came I saw I conquered," wrote Julius Caesar.

4. Jessica read books she also read magazines.

5. I wanted a new coat my old one was too small.

6. The airport was fogged-in the planes could not land.

7. Now, he regrets his comments it's too late to retract them.

8. The girls were thrilled their mothers were not.

Directions: Use a semicolon and an independent clause to complete the sentences.

9. She liked him _____

10. I chose a red shirt _____

11. Andrea sang well _____

12. She jumped for joy _____

13. Dancing is good exercise _____

14. The man was kind _____

15. The tire looked flat _____

16. My bike is missing _____

Colons

Use a **colon** . . .

   . . . after the salutation of a business letter
   . . . between the hour and the minute when showing time
   . . . between the volume and page number of a periodical
   . . . between chapters and verses of the Bible
   . . . before a list of three or more items
   . . . to introduce a long statement or quotation

> Dear Mr. Miller:
>
> I would like to place an order for five of your 1 ton scales. Please contact me, concerning price and delivery date.
>
> Sincerely,
> Ms. Jones

Examples:
   Salutation: Dear Madame:
   Hour and minute: 8:45 P.M.
   Periodical volume and page number: Newsweek 11:32
   Bible chapter and verse: John 3:16
   Before a list of three or more items: Buy these: fruit, cereal, cheese
   To introduce a long statement or quotation: Author Willa Cather said this about experiencing life: "There are only two or three human stories, and they go on repeating themselves as fiercely as if they had never happened before."

Directions: Use colons to punctuate these sentences correctly. Some sentences require more than one colon.

1. At 12 45 the president said this "Where's my lunch?"

2. Look in Proverbs 1 12 for the answer.

3. Don't forget to order these items boots, socks, shoes and leggings.

4. Ask the librarian for *Weekly Reader* 3 14.

5. Dear Sir Please send me two copies of your report.

6. Avoid these at all costs bad jokes, bad company, bad manners.

7. The statement is in either Genesis 1 6 or Exodus 3 2.

8. At 9 15 P.M., she checked in, and at 6 45 A.M., she checked out.

9. I felt all these things at once joy, anger and sadness.

10. Here's a phrase President Bush liked "A thousand points of light."

Name:_____

ENGLISH 6

Dashes

Dashes (—) are used to indicate sudden changes of thought.

Examples:
I want milk—no, make that soda—with my lunch.
Wear your old clothes—new ones would get spoiled.

Directions: If the dash is used correctly in the sentence, write **C** in the blank. If the dash is missing or used incorrectly, draw an **X** in the blank. The first one has been done for you.

_**C**___ 1. No one—not even my dad—knows about the surprise.

_____ 2. Ask—him—no I will to come to the party.

_____ 3. I'll tell you the answer oh, the phone just rang!

_____ 4. Everyone thought—even her brother—that she looked pretty.

_____ 5. Can you please—oh, forget it!

_____ 6. Just stop it I really mean it!

_____ 7. Tell her that I'll—never mind—I'll tell her myself!

_____ 8. Everyone especially Anna is overwhelmed.

_____ 9. I wish everyone could—forgive me—I'm sorry!

_____ 10. The kids—all six of them—piled into the backseat.

Directions: Write two sentences of your own that include dashes.

11. _____

_____

12. _____

_____

Quotation Marks

Quotation marks are used to enclose a speaker's exact words. Use commas to set off a direct quotation from other words in the sentence.

Examples:
  Kira smiled and said, "Quotation marks come in handy."
  "Yes," Josh said, "I'll take two."

Directions: If quotation marks and commas are used correctly, write **C** in the blank. If they are used incorrectly, write an **X** in the blank. The first one has been done for you.

___C___ 1. "I suppose," Elizabeth remarked, "that you'll be there on time."

_____ 2. "Please let me help! insisted Mark.

_____ 3. I'll be ready in 2 minutes!" her father said.

_____ 4. "Just breathe slowly," the nurse said, "and calm down."

_____ 5. "No one understands me" William whined.

_____ 6. "Would you like more milk?" Jasmine asked politely.

_____ 7. "No thanks, her grandpa replied, "I have plenty."

_____ 8. "What a beautiful morning!" Jessica yelled.

_____ 9. "Yes, it certainly is" her mother agreed.

_____ 10. "Whose purse is this?" asked Andrea.

_____ 11. It's mine" said Stephanie. "Thank you."

_____ 12. "Can you play the piano?" asked Heather.

_____ 13. "Music is my hobby." Jonathan replied.

_____ 14. Great!" yelled Harry. Let's play some tunes."

_____ 15. "I practice a lot," said Jayne proudly.

"This is exactly what I'm saying! You can tell by my quotation marks!"

Quotation Marks

Directions: Use quotation marks and commas to punctuate these sentences correctly.

"Remember: quotation marks are used to enclose a speaker's exact words."

1. No Ms. Elliot replied you may not go.

2. Watch out! yelled the coach.

3. Please bring my coat called Renee.

4. After thinking for a moment, Paul said I don't believe you.

5. Dad said Remember to be home by 9:00 P.M.

6. Finish your projects said the art instructor.

7. Go back instructed Mom and comb your hair.

8. I won't be needing my winter coat anymore replied Mei-ling.

9. He said How did you do that?

10. I stood and said My name is Rosalita.

11. No said Misha I will not attend.

12. Don't forget to put your name on your paper said the teacher.

13. Pay attention class said our history teacher.

14. As I came into the house, Mom called Dinner is almost ready!

15. Jake, come when I call you said Mother.

16. How was your trip to France Mrs. Shaw? asked Deborah.

Apostrophes

Use an **apostrophe** (') in a contraction to show that letters have been left out. A **contraction** is a shortened form of two words, usually a pronoun and a verb.

Add an **apostrophe** and **s** to form the **possessive** of singular nouns. **Plural possessives** are formed two ways. If the noun ends in **s**, simply add an apostrophe at the end of the word. If the noun does not end in **s**, add an apostrophe and **s**.

Examples:
   Contraction: He **can't** button his sleeves.
   Singular possessive: The **boy's** sleeves are too short.
   Plural noun ending in s: The **ladies'** voices were pleasant.
   Plural noun not ending in s: The **children's** song was long.

Directions: Use apostrophes to punctuate the sentences correctly. The first one has been done for you.

1. I can't understand that child's game.

2. The farmers wagons were lined up in a row.

3. She didnt like the chairs covers.

4. Our parents beliefs are often our own.

5. Sandys mothers aunt isnt going to visit.

6. Two ladies from work didnt show up.

7. The citizens group wasnt very happy.

8. The colonists demands werent unreasonable.

9. The mothers babies cried at the same time.

10. Our parents generation enjoys music.

Directions: Write two sentences of your own that include apostrophes.

11. _____

_____

12. _____

_____

Name: _____

Singular Possessives

Directions: Write the singular possessive form of each word. Then, add a noun to show possession. The first one has been done for you.

1. spider   *spider's web* _____

2. clock _____

3. car _____

4. book _____

5. Mom _____

6. boat _____

7. table _____

8. baby _____

9. woman _____

10. writer _____

11. mouse _____

12. fan _____

13. lamp _____

14. dog _____

15. boy _____

16. house _____

Name: _____

Plural Possessives

Directions: Write the plural possessive form of each word. Then add a noun to show possession. The first one has been done for you.

1. kid   <u>kids' skates</u> _____

2. man _____

3. aunt _____

4. lion _____

5. giraffe _____

6. necklace _____

7. mouse _____

8. team _____

9. clown _____

10. desk _____

11. woman _____

12. worker _____

Directions: Write three sentences of your own that include plural possessives.

13. _____

_____

14. _____

_____

15. _____

_____

Contractions

Examples:
he will = **he'll**
she is = **she's**
they are = **they're**
can not = **can't**

Contraction Chart

Pronoun		Verb		Contraction
I	+	am	=	I'm
we, you, they	+	are	=	we're, you're, they're
he, she, it	+	is	=	he's, she's, it's
I, we, you, they	+	have	=	I've, we've, you've, they've
I, you, we, she, he, they	+	would	=	I'd, you'd, we'd, she'd, he'd, they'd
I, you, we, she, he, they	+	will	=	I'll, you'll, we'll, she'll, he'll, they'll

Directions: Write a sentence using a contraction. The first one has been done for you.

1. I will   _I'll see you tomorrow!_ _____

2. they are   _____

3. we have   _____

4. she would   _____

5. you are   _____

6. they will   _____

7. she is   _____

8. he would   _____

9. they are   _____

10. I am   _____

Name: _____

Italics

Use **italics** or **underlining** for titles of books, newspapers, plays, magazines and movies.

Examples:
  Book: Have you read *Gone with the Wind*?
  Movie: Did you see *The Muppet Movie*?
  Newspaper: I like to read *The New York Times*.
  Magazine: Some children read *Sports Illustrated*.
  Play: *A Doll's House* is a play by Henrik Ibsen.

Since we cannot write in italics, we underline words that should be in italics.

Directions: Underline the words that should be in italics. The first one has been done for you.

1. I read about a play titled <u>Cats</u> in <u>The Cleveland Plain Dealer</u>.

2. You can find The New York Times in most libraries.

3. Audrey Wood wrote Elbert's Bad Word.

4. Parents and Newsweek are both popular magazines.

5. The original Miracle on 34th Street was filmed long ago.

6. Cricket and Ranger Rick are magazines for children.

7. Bon Appetit means "good appetite" and is a cooking magazine.

8. Harper's, The New Yorker and Vanity Fair are magazines.

9. David Copperfield was written by Charles Dickens.

10. Harriet Beecher Stowe wrote Uncle Tom's Cabin.

11. Paul Newman was in a movie called The Sting.

12. Have you read Ramona the Pest by Beverly Cleary?

13. The Louisville Courier Journal is a Kentucky newspaper.

14. Teen and Boy's Life are magazines for young readers.

15. Have you seen Jimmy Stewart in It's a Wonderful Life?

Name:_____

Capitalization

A. Lincoln

Capitalize . . .

. . . the first word in a sentence
. . . the first letter of a person's name
. . . proper nouns, like the names of planets, oceans and mountain ranges
. . . titles when used with a person's name, even if abbreviated (Dr., Mr., Lt.)
. . . days of the week and months of the year
. . . cities, states and countries

Directions: Write **C** in the blank if the word or phrase is capitalized correctly. Rewrite the word or phrase if it is incorrect.

1. _____ President Abraham Lincoln _____

2. _____ Larry D. Walters _____

3. _____ saturn _____

4. _____ benjamin franklin _____

5. _____ August _____

6. _____ professional _____

7. _____ jupiter _____

8. _____ Pacific Ocean _____

9. _____ white house _____

10. _____ pet _____

11. _____ Congress _____

12. _____ Houston _____

13. _____ federal government _____

14. _____ dr. Samuel White _____

15. _____ milwaukee, Wisconsin _____

16. _____ Appalachian mountains _____

17. _____ lake michigan _____

18. _____ Notre Dame College _____

19. _____ department of the Interior _____

20. _____ monday and Tuesday _____

© 1999 American Education Publishing Co.

Review

Directions: Write a sentence using each type of punctuation correctly.

1. Semicolon _____

_____

2. Colon _____

_____

3. Apostrophe in a contraction _____

_____

4. Comma _____

_____

5. Quotation marks _____

_____

6. Apostrophe (singular possessive) _____

_____

7. Apostrophe (plural possessive) _____

_____

8. Italics _____

_____

Directions: Rewrite this sentence using correct capitalization and punctuation.

9. well said lisa its about time you came back from florida i expected you last tuesday

_____

_____

Name: _____

Review

Directions: Use semicolons to punctuate these sentences correctly.

1. I said yes she said no.
2. He liked her she felt differently.
3. It's hard to say I don't know why.

Directions: Use colons to punctuate these sentences correctly.

4. At 10 45 P.M., the baby was still awake.
5. The article is in *Weekly Reader* 13 41.
6. Please order these paper, pencils, pens and chalk.

Directions: Use dashes to punctuate these sentences correctly.

7. We all especially Frank felt overjoyed.
8. No one least of all me expected the surprise.
9. Our grandmothers both of them opened their gifts.

Directions: Use commas to punctuate these sentences correctly.

10. Yes I'll put your name on the list.
11. Jessica their youngest daughter was beautiful.
12. He wanted catsup tomatoes and lettuce on his burger.

Directions: Use quotation marks to punctuate these sentences correctly.

13. I'll go! shouted Matthew. I like errands.
14. Will you please, snarled her brother, just be quiet!

Directions: Use apostrophes to punctuate these sentences correctly.

15. The ladies bonnets werent very colorful.
16. Our childrens names are special to us.

Directions: Underline the words that should be in italics.

17. Her favorite movie was The Wizard of Oz.
18. Have you read Sixes and Sevens by O. Henry?

Root Words

A **root word** is the common stem that gives related words their basic meanings.

Example: Separate is the root word for **separately**, **separation**, **inseparable** and **separator**.

Directions: Identify the root word in each group of words. Look up the meaning of the root word in the dictionary and write its definition. The first one has been done for you.

1. colorless, colorful, discolor, coloration

   Root word: _____ *color* _____

   Definition: *any coloring matter, dye, pigment or paint*

2. creator, creation, creating, creative, recreate

   Root word: _____

   Definition: _____

3. remove, movement, movable, immovable, removable

   Root word: _____

   Definition: _____

4. contentment, malcontent, discontent, discontentment

   Root word: _____

   Definition: _____

5. pleasure, displeasure, pleasing, pleasant, unpleasant

   Root word: _____

   Definition: _____

6. successor, unsuccessful, successful

   Root word: _____

   Definition: _____

Suffixes

A **suffix** is a syllable added to the end of a root word that changes its meaning.

When a word ends in silent **e**, keep the **e** before adding a suffix beginning with a consonant.

Example: amuse + ment = amusement

Exception: argue + ment = argument

When a word ends in silent **e**, drop the **e** before adding a suffix beginning with a vowel.

Example: amuse = amusing

Exceptions: hoeing, shoeing, canoeing

Directions: Write **C** on the blank if the word in bold is spelled correctly. Draw an **X** in the blank if it is spelled incorrectly. The first one has been done for you.

_C_ 1. She was a woman of many **achievements**.

____ 2. He hated to hear their **arguments**.

____ 3. Do you want to go **canoing**?

____ 4. He kept **urgeing** her to eat more dessert.

____ 5. She was not good at **deceiving** others.

____ 6. He **rarely** skipped lunch.

____ 7. Would you repeat that **announcment**?

____ 8. Bicycle **safety** was very important to him.

____ 9. Their constant **argueing** got on my nerves.

____ 10. He found that **shoeing** horses was not easy.

____ 11. The sun felt hot as they were **hoeing**.

____ 12. She was so **relieveed** that she laughed.

Suffixes: Words Ending in Y

If a word ends in a vowel and **y**, keep the **y** when you add a suffix.

Example:
    bray + ed = brayed
    bray + ing = braying

Exception: lay + ed = laid

If a word ends in a consonant and **y**, change the **y** to **i** when you add a suffix unless the suffix begins with **i**.

Example:
    baby + ed = babied
    baby + ing = babying

Directions: Write **C** in the blank if the word in bold is spelled correctly. Draw an **X** if it is spelled incorrectly. The first one has been done for you.

_C_ 1. She was a good student who did well at her **studies**.

____ 2. Will you please stop **babiing** him?

____ 3. She **layed** her purse on the couch.

____ 4. Both the **ferrys** left on schedule.

____ 5. Could you repeat what he was **saying**?

____ 6. He was **triing** to do his best.

____ 7. How many **cherries** are in this pie?

____ 8. The cat **stayed** away for two weeks.

____ 9. He is **saveing** all his money.

____ 10. The lake was **muddier** than I remembered.

____ 11. It was the **muddyest** lake I've ever seen!

____ 12. Her mother **babied** her when she was sick.

Name: _____

Suffixes: Doubling Final Consonants

a one-syllable word ends in one vowel and consonant, double the last consonant when
ou add a suffix that begins with a vowel.

xamples: swim + ing = swimming   big + er = bigger

Directions: Add the suffixes shown to the root words, doubling the final consonants when
appropriate. The first one has been done for you.

1. brim   +   ing   =   **brimming** _____

2. big   +   est   =   _____

3. hop   +   ing   =   _____

4. swim   +   er   =   _____

5. thin   +   er   =   _____

6. spin   +   ing   =   _____

7. smack   +   ing   =   _____

8. sink   +   ing   =   _____

9. win   +   er   =   _____

10. thin   +   est   =   _____

11. slim   +   er   =   _____

12. slim   +   ing   =   _____

13. thread   +   ing   =   _____

14. thread   +   er   =   _____

15. win   +   ing   =   _____

16. sing   +   ing   =   _____

17. stop   +   ing   =   _____

18. thrill   +   ing   =   _____

19. drop   +   ed   =   _____

20. mop   +   ing   =   _____

Suffixes: Doubling Final Consonants

When two-syllable words have the accent on the second syllable and end in a consonant preceded by a vowel, double the final consonant to add a suffix that begins with a vowel.

Examples: occur + ing = occurring   occur + ed = occurred

If the accent shifts to the first syllable when the suffix is added to the two-syllable root word, the final consonant is not doubled.

Example: refer + ence = reference

Directions: Say the words listed to hear where the accent falls when the suffix is added. Then add the suffix to the root word, doubling the final consonant when appropriate. The first one has been done for you.

1. excel   +   ence   = ___excellence___
2. infer   +   ing   = _____
3. regret   +   able   = _____
4. control +   able   = _____
5. submit   +   ing   = _____
6. confer   +   ing   = _____
7. refer   +   al   = _____
8. differ   +   ing   = _____
9. compel   +   ing   = _____
10. commit   +   ed   = _____
11. regret   +   ing   = _____
12. depend   +   able   = _____
13. upset   +   ing   = _____
14. propel   +   ing   = _____
15. repel   +   ed   = _____
16. prefer   +   ing   = _____
17. prefer   +   ence   = _____
18. differ   +   ence   = _____
19. refer   +   ing   = _____
20. control +   ing   = _____

EXCEL + ENCE = EXCELLENCE

Spelling: I Before E, Except After C

Use an **i** before **e**, except after **c** or when **e** and **i** together sound like long **a**.

Examples:
relieve
deceive
neighbor

Exceptions: weird, foreign, height, seize

Directions: Write **C** in the blank if the word in bold is spelled correctly. Draw an **X** in the blank if it is spelled incorrectly. The first one has been done for you.

i before e,
except after c,
or when sounding like a,
as in "neighbor" and "weigh"

C 1. They stopped at the crossing for the **freight** train.

____ 2. How much does that **wiegh**?

____ 3. Did you **believe** his story?

____ 4. He **recieved** an A on his paper!

____ 5. She said it was the **nieghborly** thing to do.

____ 6. The guards **seized** the package.

____ 7. That movie was **wierd**!

____ 8. Her **hieght** is five feet, six inches.

____ 9. It's not right to **deceive** others.

____ 10. Your answers should be **breif**.

____ 11. She felt a lot of **grief** when her dog died.

____ 12. He is still **greiving** about his loss.

____ 13. Did the police catch the **thief**?

____ 14. She was their **cheif** source of information.

____ 15. Can you speak a **foreign** language?

Name:_____

Spelling: The Letter Q

In English words, the letter **q** is always followed by the letter **u**.

Examples:
　question
　square
　quick

Directions: Write the correct spelling of each word in the blank. The first one has been done for you.

1. qill _____quill_____

2. eqality _____

3. qarrel _____

4. qarter _____

5. qart _____

6. qibble _____

7. qench _____

8. qeen _____

9. qip _____

10. qiz _____

11. eqipment _____

12. qiet _____

13. qite _____

14. eqity _____

15. eqator _____

16. eqivalent _____

17. eqitable _____

18. eqestrian _____

19. eqation _____

20. qantity _____

QUARTERS
QUALITY
QUIET

EQUAL
ACQUIRE
EQUATOR

Prefixes

A **prefix** is a syllable added to the beginning of a word that changes its meaning. The prefixes **in**, **il**, **ir** and **im** all mean **not**.

Directions: Create new words by adding **in**, **il**, **ir** or **im** to these root words. Use a dictionary to check that the new words are correct. The first one has been done for you.

Prefix		Root Word		New Word
1. _____il_____	+	logical	=	_____illogical_____
2. _____	+	literate	=	_____
3. _____	+	patient	=	_____
4. _____	+	probable	=	_____
5. _____	+	reversible	=	_____
6. _____	+	responsible	=	_____
7. _____	+	active	=	_____
8. _____	+	moral	=	_____
9. _____	+	removable	=	_____
10. _____	+	legible	=	_____
11. _____	+	mature	=	_____
12. _____	+	perfect	=	_____

Name: _____

Prefixes

The prefixes **un** and **non** also mean **not**.

Examples:
    Unhappy means not happy.
    Nonproductive means not productive.

Directions: Divide each word into its prefix and root word. The first one has been done for you.

	Prefix	**Root Word**
1. unappreciated	un	appreciate
2. unlikely	_____	_____
3. unkempt	_____	_____
4. untimely	_____	_____
5. nonstop	_____	_____
6. nonsense	_____	_____
7. nonprofit	_____	_____
8. nonresident	_____	_____

Directions: Use the clues in the first sentence to complete the second sentence with one of the words from the box. The first one has been done for you.

9. She didn't reside at school. She was a ___nonresident._____

10. He couldn't stop talking. He talked _____

11. The company did not make a profit. It was a _____ company.

12. She was not talking sense. She was talking _____

13. He visited at a bad time. His visit was _____

14. No one appreciated his efforts. He felt _____

15. He did not "keep up" his hair. His hair was _____

16. She was not likely to come. Her coming was _____

Name: _____

Suffixes

The suffix **less** means **lacking** or **without**. The suffix **some** means **full** or **like**.

Examples:
  Hopeless means without hope.
  Awesome means filled with awe.

Directions: Create new words by adding **some** or **less** to these root words. Use a dictionary to check that the new words are correct. The first one has been done for you.

Root Word		Suffix		New Word
1. heart	+	less	=	heartless
2. trouble	+	_____	=	_____
3. home	+	_____	=	_____
4. humor	+	_____	=	_____
5. awe	+	_____	=	_____
6. child	+	_____	=	_____
7. win	+	_____	=	_____

Directions: Use the clues in the first sentence to complete the second sentence with one of the words from the box. The first one has been done for you.

8. Her smile was winning and delightful. She had a _____ winsome _____ smile .

9. The mean man seemed to have no heart. He was _____

10. She never smiled or laughed. She appeared to be _____

11. The solar system fills me with awe. It is _____

12. The couple had no children. They were _____

13. He had no place to live. He was _____

14. The pet caused the family trouble. It was _____

Name:_____

Suffixes

The suffix **ment** means the **act of** or **state of**. The suffixes **ible** and **able** mean **able to**.

Directions: Create new words by adding **ment** or **able** to these root words. Use a dictionary to check that the new words are correct. The first one has been done for you.

Root Word		Suffix		New Word
1. rely	+	able	=	reliable
2. retire	+	_____	=	_____
3. sense	+	_____	=	_____
4. commit	+	_____	=	_____
5. repair	+	_____	=	_____
6. love	+	_____	=	_____
7. quote	+	_____	=	_____
8. honor	+	_____	=	_____

Directions: Use the clues in the first sentence to complete the second sentence with one of the words from the box. The first one has been done for you.

9. Everyone loved her. She was _____loveable (also lovable)._____

10. He had a lot of sense. He was _____

11. She committed time to the project. She made a _____

12. He always did the right thing. His behavior was _____

13. The tire could not be fixed. It was not _____

14. They would not buy the car. The car was not _____

15. He gave the reporter good comments. His comments were _____

16. She was ready to retire. She looked forward to _____

Name: _____

Synonyms

ynonyms are words that have the same or almost the same meaning.

xamples:
  small and **little**
  big and **large**
  bright and **shiny**
  unhappy and **sad**

irections: Circle the two words in each sentence hat are synonyms. The first one has been done for you.

1. The (small) girl petted the (little) kitten.

2. I gave him a present, and she brought a gift, too.

3. She had a pretty smile and wore a beautiful sweater.

4. The huge man had enormous muscles.

5. They were not late, but we were tardy.

6. I saw a circular window with rounded glass.

7. Her eyes silently asked us to be quiet.

8. The dog was cowardly; she was really afraid of everything.

9. He wasn't rich, but everyone said he was wealthy.

10. Did you see the filthy cat with the dirty fur?

11. She's very intelligent—and her brother is smart, too.

12. He jumped over the puddle and leaped into the air.

13. The firefighters came quickly, but the fire was already burning rapidly.

14. She said the baby was cute and smiled at the infant.

15. He threw a rock, and she kicked at a stone.

Antonyms

Antonyms are words that have opposite meanings.

Examples:
   big and **little**
   pretty and **ugly**
   common and **uncommon**
   short and **tall**

awful	broad	cooked	inactive	dull
enemy	happy	smooth	stale	tardy
tiny	war	whisper	wonderful	wrong

Directions: Using words from the box, write the correct antonyms for the words in bold. The first one has been done for you.

1. It was hard to walk on the **narrow** streets.   **broad** _____

2. He was an **enormous** person. _____

3. Her answer was **correct**. _____

4. The boy said he was **despondent**. _____

5. The fabric felt **rough** to her touch. _____

6. His sense of humor was very **sharp**. _____

7. The soup tasted **awful**. _____

8. She always ate **raw** carrots. _____

9. He insisted the bread was **fresh**. _____

10. His singing voice was **wonderful**. _____

11. She was always **on time**. _____

12. The butterfly was **lively**. _____

13. His **shout** was unintentional. _____

14. He is my **friend**. _____

15. "This is a time of **peace**," the statesman said. _____

Name: _____

Review

Directions: Spell these silent **e** words correctly.

1. achievments   _____

2. canoing   _____

3. amuseing   _____

4. urgeing   _____

Directions: Add the suffixes to these words ending in **y** and spell them correctly.

5. baby + ies =   _____

6. stay + ed =   _____

Directions: Add the suffixes and spell these one-syllable words correctly.

7. hope + ing =   _____

8. stop + ing =   _____

Directions: Add the suffixes and spell these two-syllable words correctly.

9. recur + ing =   _____

10. defer + ence =   _____

Directions: Spell these words correctly by inserting **ie** or **ei**.

11. h __ __ ght

12. ch __ __ f

Directions: Circle the **q** words in each row that are spelled correctly.

13. quip	qeen	qick	quit
14. qestion	equator	quiet	qart
15. squirrel	sqare	squirm	sqeak

Name: _____

Review

Directions: Use these words with prefixes and suffixes in sentences of your own.

1. prepackaged _____

   _____

   _____

2. underground _____

   _____

3. fixable _____

   _____

4. excitement _____

   _____

5. restless _____

   _____

Directions: Write three sets of antonyms.

6. _____   _____

7. _____   _____

8. _____   _____

Directions: Write three sets of synonyms.

9. _____   _____

10. _____   _____

11. _____   _____

Name:_____

Review

Directions: Add the prefix **un** or **non** to these root words.

1. friendly _____

2. sense _____

3. profit _____

4. known _____

Directions: Add the suffix **less**, **ment** or **some** to these root words.

5. awe _____

6. word _____

7. amaze _____

8. harm _____

Directions: Identify the root word in each group of words below. Write it in the blank.

9. responsive, responding, responsive _____

10. repetitive, repetition, repeatable _____

Directions: Write synonyms for these words.

11. skinny _____

12. overweight _____

13. unhappy _____

14. rainy _____

Directions: Write antonyms for these words.

15. hot _____

16. profit _____

17. sorrow _____

18. friend _____

Name: _____

"Affect" and "Effect"

Affect means to act upon or influence.

Example: Studying will **affect** my test grade.

Effect means to bring about a result or to accomplish something.

Example: The **effect** of her smile was immediate!

I HOPE ALL THIS STUDYING AFFECTS MY GRADE!

Directions: Write **affect** or **effect** in the blanks to complete these sentences correctly. The first one has been done for you.

__affects__ 1. Your behavior (affects/effects) how others feel about you.

_____ 2. His (affect/effect) on her was amazing.

_____ 3. The (affect/effect) of his jacket was striking.

_____ 4. What you say won't (affect/effect) me!

_____ 5. There's a relationship between cause and (affect/effect).

_____ 6. The (affect/effect) of her behavior was positive.

_____ 7. The medicine (affected/effected) my stomach.

_____ 8. What was the (affect/effect) of the punishment?

_____ 9. Did his behavior (affect/effect) her performance?

_____ 10. The cold (affected/effected) her breathing.

_____ 11. The (affect/effect) was instantaneous!

_____ 12. Your attitude will (affect/effect) your posture.

_____ 13. The (affect/effect) on her posture was major.

_____ 14. The (affect/effect) of the colored lights was calming.

_____ 15. She (affected/effected) his behavior.

Name: _____

"Among" and "Between"

Among is a preposition that applies to more than two people or things.

Example: The group divided the cookies **among** themselves.

Between is a preposition that applies to only two people or things.

Example: The cookies were divided **between** Jeremy and Sara.

WE'LL DIVIDE THESE AMONG OURSELVES!

Directions: Write **between** or **among** in the blanks to complete these sentences correctly. The first one has been done for you.

between ___ 1. The secret is (between/among) you and Jon.

_____ 2. (Between/Among) the two of them, whom do you think is nicer?

_____ 3. I must choose (between/among) the cookies, candy and pie.

_____ 4. She threaded her way (between/among) the kids on the playground.

_____ 5. She broke up a fight (between/among) Josh and Sean.

_____ 6. "What's come (between/among) you two?" she asked.

_____ 7. "I'm (between/among) a rock and a hard place," Josh responded.

_____ 8. "He has to choose (between/among) all his friends," Sean added.

_____ 9. "Are you (between/among) his closest friends?" she asked Sean.

_____ 10. "It's (between/among) another boy and me," Sean replied.

_____ 11. "Can't you settle it (between/among) the group?"

_____ 12. "No," said Josh. "This is (between/among) Sean and me."

_____ 13. "I'm not sure he's (between/among) my closest friends."

_____ 14. Sean, Josh and Andy began to argue (between/among) themselves.

_____ 15. I hope Josh won't have to choose (between/among) the two!

"All Together" and "Altogether"

All together is a phrase meaning everyone or everything in the same place.

Example: We put the eggs **all together** in the bowl.

Altogether is an adverb that means entirely, completely or in all.

Example: The teacher gave **altogether** too much homework.

THE EGGS ARE ALL TOGETHER

Directions: Write **altogether** or **all together** in the blanks to complete these sentences correctly. The first one has been done for you.

altogether	1. "You ate (altogether/all together) too much food."
_____	2. The girls sat (altogether/all together) on the bus.
_____	3. (Altogether/All together) now: one, two, three!
_____	4. I am (altogether/all together) out of ideas.
_____	5. We are (altogether/all together) on this project.
_____	6. "You have on (altogether/all together) too much makeup!"
_____	7. They were (altogether/all together) on the same team.
_____	8. (Altogether/All together), we can help stop
_____	pollution (altogether/all together).
_____	9. He was not (altogether/all together) happy with his grades.
_____	10. The kids were (altogether/all together) too loud.
_____	11. (Altogether/All together), the babies cried gustily.
_____	12. She was not (altogether/all together) sure what to do.
_____	13. Let's sing the song (altogether/all together).
_____	14. He was (altogether/all together) too pushy for her taste.
_____	15. (Altogether/All together), the boys yelled the school cheer.

Name: _____

"Amount" and "Number"

Amount indicates quantity, bulk or mass.

Example: She carried a large **amount** of money in her purse.

Number indicates units.

Example: What **number** of people volunteered to work?

Directions: Write **amount** or **number** in the blanks to complete these sentences correctly. The first one has been done for you.

<u>number</u>   1. She did not (amount/number) him among her closest friends.

_____   2. What (amount/number) of ice cream should we order?

_____   3. The (amount/number) of cookies on her plate was three.

_____   4. His excuses did not (amount/number) to much.

_____   5. Her contribution (amounted/numbered) to half the money raised.

_____   6. The (amount/number) of injured players rose every day.

_____   7. What a huge (amount/number) of cereal!

_____   8. The (amount/number) of calories in the diet was low.

_____   9. I can't tell you the (amount/number) of friends she has!

_____   10. The total (amount/number) of money raised was incredible!

_____   11. The (amount/number) of gadgets for sale was amazing.

_____   12. He was startled by the (amount/number) of people present.

_____   13. He would not do it for any (amount/number) of money.

_____   14. She offered a great (amount/number) of reasons for her actions.

_____   15. Can you guess the (amount/number) of beans in the jar?

"Irritate" and "Aggravate"

Irritate means to cause impatience, to provoke or annoy.

Example: His behavior **irritated** his father.

Aggravate means to make a condition worse.

Example: Her sunburn was **aggravated** by additional exposure to the sun.

Directions: Write **aggravate** or **irritate** in the blanks to complete these sentences correctly. The first one has been done for you.

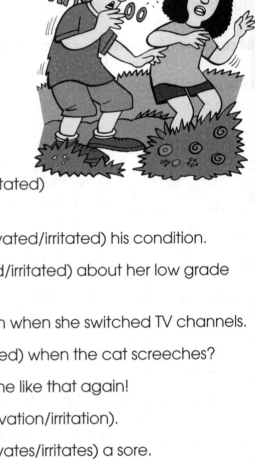

__aggravated__ 1. The weeds (aggravated/irritated) his hay fever.

_____ 2. Scratching the bite (aggravated/irritated) his condition.

_____ 3. Her father was (aggravated/irritated) about her low grade in math.

_____ 4. It (aggravated/irritated) him when she switched TV channels.

_____ 5. Are you (aggravated/irritated) when the cat screeches?

_____ 6. Don't (aggravate/irritate) me like that again!

_____ 7. He was in a state of (aggravation/irritation).

_____ 8. Picking at the scab (aggravates/irritates) a sore.

_____ 9. Whistling (aggravates/irritates) the old grump.

_____ 10. She was (aggravated/irritated) when she learned about it.

_____ 11. "Please don't (aggravate/irritate) your mother," Dad warned.

_____ 12. His asthma was (aggravated/irritated) by too much stress.

_____ 13. Sneezing is sure to (aggravate/irritate) his allergies.

_____ 14. Did you do that just to (aggravate/irritate) me?

_____ 15. Her singing always (aggravated/irritated) her brother.

Name: _____

"Principal" and "Principle"

Principal means main, leader or chief, or a sum of money that earns interest.

Examples:
The high school **principal** earned interest on the **principal** in his savings account.
The **principal** reason for his savings account was to save for retirement.

Principle means a truth, law or a moral outlook that governs the way someone behaves.

Example:
Einstein discovered some fundamental **principles** of science.
Stealing is against her **principles**.

Directions: Write **principle** or **principal** in the blanks to complete these sentences correctly.
The first one has been done for you.

principle   1. A (principle/principal) of biology is "the survival of the fittest."

_____ 2. She was a person of strong (principles/principals).

_____ 3. The (principles/principals) sat together at the district conference.

_____ 4. How much of the total in my savings account is
    (principle/principal)?

_____ 5. His hay fever was the (principle/principal) reason for his sneezing.

_____ 6. It's not the facts that upset me, it's the (principles/principals) of
    the case.

_____ 7. The jury heard only the (principle/principal) facts.

_____ 8. Our school (principle/principal) is strict but fair.

_____ 9. Spend the interest, but don't touch the (principle/principal).

_____ 10. Helping others is a guiding (principle/principal) of the
    homeless shelter.

_____ 11. In (principle/principal), we agree; on the facts, we do not.

_____ 12. The (principle/principal) course at dinner was leg of lamb.

_____ 13. Some mathematical (principles/principals) are difficult
    to understand.

_____ 14. The baby was the (principle/principal) reason for his happiness.

"Good" and "Well"

Good is always an adjective. It is used to modify a noun or pronoun.

Examples:
We enjoyed the **good** food.
We had a **good** time yesterday.
It was **good** to see her again.

Well is used to modify verbs, to describe someone's health or to describe how someone is dressed.

Examples:
I feel **well**. He looked **well**.
He was **well**-dressed for the weather.
She sang **well**.

Directions: Write **good** or **well** in the blanks to complete these sentences correctly.

1. She performed _____.

2. You look _____ in that color.

3. These apples are _____.

4. He rides his bike _____.

5. She made a _____ attempt to win the race.

6. The man reported that all was _____ in the coal mine.

7. Jonas said, "I feel _____, thank you."

8. The team played _____.

9. Mom fixed a _____ dinner.

10. The teacher wrote, " _____ work!" on top of my paper.

Name: _____

"Like" and "As"

Like means something is similar, resembles something else or describes how things are similar in manner.

Examples:
   She could sing **like** an angel.
   She looks **like** an angel, too!

As is a conjunction, a joining word, that links two independent clauses in a sentence.

Example: He felt chilly **as** night fell.

Sometimes **as** precedes an independent clause.

Example: As I told you, I will not be at the party.

Directions: Write **like** or **as** in the blanks to complete these sentences correctly. The first one has been done for you.

___as___   1. He did not behave (like/as) I expected.

_____   2. She was (like/as) a sister to me.

_____   3. The puppy acted (like/as) a baby!

_____   4. (Like/As) I was saying, he will be there at noon.

_____   5. The storm was 25 miles away, (like/as) he predicted.

_____   6. He acted exactly (like/as) his father.

_____   7. The song sounds (like/as) a hit to me!

_____   8. Grandpa looked (like/as) a much younger man.

_____   9. (Like/As) I listened to the music, I grew sleepy.

_____ 10. (Like/As) I expected, he showed up late.

_____ 11. She dances (like/as) a ballerina!

_____ 12. (Like/As) she danced, the crowd applauded.

_____ 13. On stage, she looks (like/as) a professional!

_____ 14. (Like/As) I thought, she has taken lessons for years.

Review

Directions: Use these words in sentences of your own.

1. affect _____

   _____

2. effect _____

   _____

3. among _____

   _____

4. between _____

   _____

5. irritate _____

   _____

6. aggravate _____

   _____

7. principal _____

   _____

8. principle _____

   _____

9. good _____

   _____

10. well _____

    _____

11. like _____

    _____

12. as _____

    _____

Review

Directions: Write the correct word in the blank.

_____ 1. The (affect/effect) of the shot was immediate.

_____ 2. The shot (affected/effected) her allergies.

_____ 3. You have a positive (affect/effect) on me!

_____ 4. I was deeply (affected/effected) by the speech.

_____ 5. The prize was shared (among/between) Art and Lisa.

_____ 6. She was (among/between) the best students in the class.

_____ 7. He felt he was (among/between) friends.

_____ 8. It was hard to choose (among/between) all the gifts.

_____ 9. Does it (irritate/aggravate) you to see people smoke?

_____ 10. Does smoking (irritate/aggravate) his sore throat?

_____ 11. He wondered why she was (irritated/aggravated) at him.

_____ 12. The intensity of his (irritation/aggravation) grew each day.

_____ 13. She had a (principal/principle) part in the play.

_____ 14. Beans were the (principal/principle) food in his diet.

_____ 15. She was a woman of strong (principals/principles).

_____ 16. Mr. Larson was their favorite (principal/principle).

_____ 17. The (amount/number) of ice-cream cones he ate was incredible.

_____ 18. I wouldn't part with it for any (amount/number) of money.

_____ 19. It happened exactly (like/as) I had predicted!

_____ 20. He sounds almost (like/as) his parents.

Name: _____

Types of Analogies

An **analogy** shows similarities, or things in common, between a pair of words. The relationships between the words in analogies usually fall into these categories:

1. **Purpose**   One word in the pair shows the **purpose** of the other word (scissors: cut).

2. **Antonyms**   The words are **opposites** (light: dark).

3. **Part/whole**   One word in the pair is a **part**; the other is a **whole** (leg: body).

4. **Action/object** One word in the pair involves an **action** with or to an **object** (fly: airplane).

5. **Association**   One word in the pair is what you think of or **associate** when you see the other (cow: milk).

6. **Object/location** One word in the pair tells the **location** of where the other word, an **object**, is found (car: garage).

7. **Cause/effect**   One word in the pair tells the **cause**; the other word shows the **effect** (practice: improvement).

8. **Synonyms**   The words are **synonyms** (small: tiny).

Directions: Write the relationship between the words in each pair. The first two have been done for you.

1. cow: farm   _____object/location_____
2. toe: foot   _____part/whole_____
3. watch: TV   _____
4. bank: money   _____
5. happy: unhappy   _____
6. listen: radio   _____
7. inning: ballgame   _____
8. knife: cut   _____
9. safe: dangerous   _____
10. carrots: soup   _____

Name:_____

Writing Analogies

Once you have determined the relationship between the words in the first pair, the next step is to find a similar relationship between another pair of words.

Examples:
Scissors is to **cut** as **broom** is to **sweep**.
Black is to **white** as **up** is to **down**.

Scissors cut. Brooms sweep. The first analogy shows the **purpose** of scissors and brooms. In the second example, up and down are **antonyms**, as are black and white.

Directions: Choose the correct word to complete each analogy. The first one has been done for you.

1. **Sky** is to **blue** as **grass** is to
   A. earth   B. green   C. lawn   D. yard   ___green___

2. **Snow** is to **winter** as **rain** is to
   A. umbrella   B. wet   C. slicker   D. spring   _____

3. **Sun** is to **day** as **moon** is to
   A. dark   B. night   C. stars   D. blackness   _____

4. **5** is to **10** as **15** is to
   A. 50   B. 25   C. 30   D. 40   _____

5. **Collie** is to **dog** as **Siamese** is to
   A. pet   B. kitten   C. baby   D. cat   _____

6. **Letter** is to **word** as **note** is to
   A. tuba   B. music   C. instruments   D. singer   _____

7. **100** is to **10** as **1,000** is to
   A. 10   B. 200   C. 100   D. 10,000   _____

8. **Back** is to **rear** as **pit** is to
   A. peach   B. hole   C. dark   D. punishment   _____

Name:_____

Analogies of Purpose

Directions: Choose the correct word to complete each analogy of purpose. The first one has been done for you.

1. **Knife** is to **cut** as **copy machine** is to

   A. duplicate　　B. paper　　C. copies　　D. office　　___duplicate___

2. **Bicycle** is to **ride** as **glass** is to

   A. dishes　　B. dinner　　C. drink　　D. break　　_____

3. **Hat** is to **cover** as **eraser** is to

   A. chalkboard　B. pencil　　C. mistake　　D. erase　　_____

4. **Mystery** is to **clue** as **door** is to

   A. house　　B. key　　C. window　　D. open　　_____

5. **Television** is to **see** as **CD** is to

   A. sound　　B. hear　　C. play　　D. dance　　_____

6. **Clock** is to **time** as **ruler** is to

   A. height　　B. length　　C. measure　　D. inches　　_____

7. **Fry** is to **pan** as **bake** is to

   A. cookies　　B. dinner　　C. oven　　D. baker　　_____

8. **Bowl** is to **fruit** as **wrapper** is to

   A. present　　B. candy　　C. paper　　D. ribbon　　_____

Name: _____

Antonym Analogies

Directions: Write antonyms for these words.

1. run: _____

2. start: _____

3. laugh: _____

4. dependent: _____

5. young: _____

6. North: _____

7. sink: _____

8. success: _____

9. combine: _____

10. laugh: _____

11. polluted: _____

12. leader: _____

13. fascinate: _____

14. man: _____

15. awake: _____

16. begin: _____

17. increase: _____

18. reverse: _____

19. enlarge: _____

20. East: _____

21. rural: _____

22. amateur: _____

23. patient: _____

24. rich: _____

25. empty: _____

26. fancy: _____

27. introduction: _____

28. modern: _____

Directions: Write two antonym analogies of your own.

29. _____

_____

30. _____

_____

Name: _____

Part/Whole Analogies

Directions: Determine whether each analogy is whole to part or part to whole by studying the relationship between the first pair of words. Then choose the correct word to complete each analogy. The first one has been done for you.

1. **Shoestring** is to **shoe** as **brim** is to

   A. cup   B. shade   C. hat   D. scarf   ____hat____

2. **Egg** is to **yolk** as **suit** is to

   A. clothes   B. shoes   C. business   D. jacket   _____

3. **Stanza** is to **poem** as **verse** is to

   A. rhyme   B. singing   C. song   D. music   _____

4. **Wave** is to **ocean** as **branch** is to

   A. stream   B. lawn   C. office   D. tree   _____

5. **Chicken** is to **farm** as **giraffe** is to

   A. animal   B. zoo   C. tall   D. stripes   _____

6. **Finger** is to **nail** as **leg** is to

   A. arm   B. torso   C. knee   D. walk   _____

7. **Player** is to **team** as **inch** is to

   A. worm   B. measure   C. foot   D. short   _____

8. **Peak** is to **mountain** as **crest** is to

   A. wave   B. ocean   C. beach   D. water   _____

ENGLISH 6

Action/Object Analogies

Directions: Determine whether each analogy is action/object or object/action by studying the relationship between the first pair of words. Then choose the correct word to complete each analogy. The first one has been done for you.

Mow is to **grass** as **shear** is to

  A. cut   B. fleece   C. sheep   D. barber   ___**sheep**___

Rod is to **fishing** as **gun** is to

  A. police   B. crime   C. shoot   D. hunting   _____

Ship is to **captain** as **airplane** is to

  A. fly   B. airport   C. pilot   D. passenger   _____

Car is to **mechanic** as **body** is to

  A. patient   B. doctor   C. torso   D. hospital   _____

Cheat is to **exam** as **swindle** is to

  A. criminal   B. business   C. crook   D. crime   _____

Actor is to **stage** as **surgeon** is to

  A. patient   B. hospital   C. operating room D. knife   _____

Ball is to **throw** as **knife** is to

  A. cut   B. spoon   C. dinner   D. silverware   _____

Lawyer is to **trial** as **surgeon** is to

  A. patient   B. hospital   C. operation   D. operating room _____

Name: _____

Analogies of Association

Directions: Choose the correct word to complete each analogy. The first one has been done for you.

1. **Flowers** are to **spring** as **leaves** are to

   A. rakes   B. trees   C. fall   D. green   _____fall_____

2. **Ham** is to **eggs** as **butter** is to

   A. fat   B. toast   C. breakfast   D. spread   _____

3. **Bat** is to **swing** as **ball** is to

   A. throw   B. dance   C. base   D. soft   _____

4. **Chicken** is to **egg** as **cow** is to

   A. barn   B. calf   C. milk   D. beef   _____

5. **Bed** is to **sleep** as **chair** is to

   A. sit   B. couch   C. relax   D. table   _____

6. **Cube** is to **square** as **sphere** is to

   A. circle   B. triangle   C. hemisphere   D. spear   _____

7. **Kindness** is to **friend** as **cruelty** is to

   A. meanness   B. enemy   C. war   D. unkindness   _____

8. **Pumpkin** is to **pie** as **chocolate** is to

   A. cake   B. dark   C. taste   D. dessert   _____

Name: _____

Object/Location Analogies

Directions: Write a location word for each object.

1. shirt: _____

2. milk: _____

3. vase: _____

4. screwdriver: _____

5. cow: _____

6. chalkboard: _____

7. shower: _____

8. cucumbers: _____

9. silverware: _____

10. car: _____

11. pages: _____

12. bees: _____

13. money: _____

14. salt water: _____

15. dress: _____

16. ice cream: _____

17. table: _____

18. medicine: _____

19. dog: _____

20. basketball: _____

21. bed: _____

22. roses: _____

23. dishwasher: _____

24. toys: _____

25. cookies: _____

26. bird: _____

27. seashells: _____

28. asteroids: _____

Cause/Effect Analogies

Directions: Determine whether the analogy is cause/effect or effect/cause by studying the relationship between the first pair of words. Then choose the correct word to complete each analogy. The first one has been done for you.

You caused this...and now look at the effect!

1. **Ashes** are to **flame** as **darkness** is to

   A. light   B. daylight   C. eclipse   D. sun   _eclipse_

2. **Strong** is to **exercising** as **elected** is to

   A. office   B. senator   C. politician   D. campaigning   _____

3. **Fall** is to **pain** as **disobedience** is to

   A. punishment B. morals   C. behavior   D. carelessness   _____

4. **Crying** is to **sorrow** as **smiling** is to

   A. teeth   B. mouth   C. joy   D. friends   _____

5. **Germ** is to **disease** as **war** is to

   A. soldiers   B. enemies   C. destruction D. tanks   _____

6. **Distracting** is to **noise** as **soothing** is to

   A. balm   B. warmth   C. hugs   D. music   _____

7. **Food** is to **nutrition** as **light** is to

   A. vision   B. darkness   C. sunshine   D. bulb   _____

8. **Clouds** are to **rain** as **winds** are to

   A. springtime B. hurricanes   C. clouds   D. March   _____

Synonym Analogies

Name:_____

Directions: Write synonyms for these words.

1. miniature: _____

2. wind: _____

3. picture: _____

4. quiet: _____

5. run: _____

6. cloth: _____

7. mean: _____

8. cup: _____

9. sweet: _____

10. difficult: _____

11. obey: _____

12. plenty: _____

13. scent: _____

14. sudden: _____

15. gigantic: _____

16. rain: _____

17. cabinet: _____

18. loud: _____

19. leap: _____

20. jeans: _____

21. kind: _____

22. dish: _____

23. feline: _____

24. simple: _____

25. beautiful: _____

26. scorch: _____

27. story: _____

28. thaw: _____

Directions: Write two synonym analogies of your own.

29. _____

_____

_____

30. _____

_____

_____

Name:_____

Review

Directions: Name the type of analogy represented by each pair of words.

1. spoon: stir   _____

2. above: beneath   _____

3. Thanksgiving: turkey   _____

4. flour: cookies   _____

5. pollen: sneeze   _____

6. horse: barn   _____

Directions: Choose the correct word to complete each analogy.

1. **Paint** is to **artist** as **clay** is to

   A. pots   B. dirt   C. bricks   D. potter   _____

2. **Mumble** is to **talk** as **scrawl** is to

   A. paper   B. pen   C. signature   D. write   _____

3. **Whisper** is to **quiet** as **screech** is to

   A. disturbing   B. silent   C. loud   D. shriek   _____

4. **Land** is to **sea** as **dry** is to

   A. paper   B. wet   C. sand   D. eyes   _____

94

Similes

A **simile** compares two things that are not alike.
The words **like** or **as** are used to make the comparison.

Examples:

Her eyes sparkled **like** stars.
He was as kind **as** a saint.

Directions: Complete the similes. The first one has
been done for you.

1. Mason was as angry as ___a snapping turtle._____

2. His smile was like _____

3. The baby cried like _____

4. I am as happy as _____

5. The dog barked like _____

6. Her voice was like _____

7. The children were as restless as _____

8. My heart felt like _____

9. The sunshine looked like _____

10. The river was as deep as _____

11. The black clouds looked like _____

12. Her words sounded like _____

13. My eyes flashed like _____

14. His smile was as bright as _____

15. The fog was like _____

Name: _____

Metaphors

A **metaphor** is a type of comparison that says one thing *is* another. Depending on the tense used, **was** and **are** may also be used in a metaphor. The words **like** or **as** are not used in a metaphor.

Examples:

> The boy's skinny legs **are sticks**.
> Her smile was a **ray of sunshine**.

Use nouns in your comparison. Do not use adverbs or adjectives. A metaphor says one thing *is* another. The other thing must also be a noun. A metaphor is not literally true. That is why it is called a type of "figurative language."

Example:

> **Correct:** The sunshine is a **blanket** of warmth. **Blanket** is a noun.
> **Incorrect:** The sunshine is **warm**. **Warm** is an adjective.

Directions: Complete the metaphors. The first one has been done for you.

1. In the evening, the sun is a/an ___big, bright penny.___

2. At night, the moon is a/an _____

3. When you're sad, a friend is a/an _____

4. My mother is a/an _____

5. The doctor was a/an _____

6. The peaceful lake is a/an _____

7. Her pesky dog is a/an _____

8. His vivid imagination was a/an _____

9. Our vacation was a/an _____

10. The twisting, narrow road is a/an _____

11. The constantly buzzing fly is a/an _____

12. The smiling baby is a/an _____

13. His straight white teeth are a/an _____

14. The bright blue sky is a/an _____

15. The soft green grass is a/an _____

© 1999 American Education Publishing Co.

Poetry

Format:
Line 1: Name
Line 2: Name is a (metaphor)
Line 3: He/she is like (simile)
Line 4: He/she (three action words)
Line 5: He/she (relationship)
Line 6: Name

Example:
Jessica
Jessica is a joy.
She is like a playful puppy.
She tumbles, runs and laughs.
She's my baby sister!
Jessica

Directions: Build a poem that describes a friend or relative by using similes, metaphors and other words of your choice. Follow the form of the example poem.

_____

_____

_____

_____

_____

Name: _____

Poetry: Haiku

Haiku is a type of unrhymed Japanese poetry with three lines. The first line has five syllables. The second line has seven syllables. The third line has five syllables.

Example:

Katie

Katie is my dog.
She likes to bark and chase balls.
Katie is my friend.

Directions: Write a haiku about a pet and another about a hobby you enjoy. Be sure to write a title on the first line.

Pet   _____

_____

_____

_____

Hobby   _____

_____

_____

_____

98

Name:_____

Poetry: Diamanté

A **diamanté** is a poem in the shape of a diamond. Diamantés have seven lines with this format:

Line 1: one-word noun, opposite of word in line 7
Line 2: two adjectives describing line 1
Line 3: three **ing** or **ed** words about line 1
Line 4: two nouns about line 1 and two nouns about line 7
Line 5: three **ing** or **ed** words about line 7
Line 6: two adjectives describing line 7
Line 7: one word noun, opposite of word in line 1

Example:

child
happy, playful
running, singing, laughing
toys, games, job, family
working, driving, nurturing
responsible, busy
adult

Directions: Write a diamanté of your own.

_____

_____

_____

_____

_____

_____

© 1999 American Education Publishing Co.

Friendly Letters

Directions: Study the format for writing a letter to a friend. Then answer the questions.

your return address	123 Waverly Road
	Cincinnati, Ohio 45241
date	June 23, 1999
greeting	Dear Josh,
body	How is your summer going? I am enjoying mine so far. I have been swimming twice already this week, and it's only Wednesday! I am glad there is a pool near our house.
	My parents said that you can stay overnight when your family comes for the 4th of July picnic. Do you want to? We can pitch a tent in the back yard and camp out. It will be a lot of fun!
	Please write back to let me know if you can stay over on the 4th. I will see you then!
closing	Your friend,
signature	Michael

your return address	Michael Delaney
	123 Waverly Road
	Cincinnati, Ohio 45241
main address	Josh Sommers
	2250 West First Ave.
	Columbus, OH 43212

1. What words are in the greeting? _____

2. What words are in the closing?_____

3. On what street does the writer live? _____

Name: _____

Friendly Letters

Directions: Follow the format for writing a letter to a friend. Don't forget to address the envelope!

Review

Directions: Write **metaphor** or **simile** in the blanks.

1. She's an angel!   _____

2. He sings like a bird.   _____

3. My sister is a snake.   _____

4. The baby sleeps like a kitten.   _____

Directions: Label the parts of this friendly letter.

_____

_____

_____

_____

_____

_____

_____

_____

2250 West First Ave.
Columbus, Ohio 43212
June 30, 1999

Dear Michael,

   Sounds like you are having a great summer! I have been swimming, too, but not as often as you have! Maybe we can go swimming on the 4th after our families have the picnic. My mom and dad said I could stay over and camp with you. I will take the bus home the next afternoon. I will bring my sleeping bag and a lantern for us to use to scare off any bears, hah, hah.
   See you next week!

                    Your friend,
                    Josh

Josh Sommers
2250 West First Ave.
Columbus, OH 43212

                    Michael Delaney
                    123 Waverly Road
                    Cincinnati, Ohio 45241

Name:_____

Cumulative Review

Directions: Identify the part of speech of the words in bold.
The first one has been done for you.

preposition

1. The dog ran **across** the field. _____preposition_____

2. My **parents** allow me to stay up until 10:00 P.M. _____

3. Our cat **is** long-haired. _____

4. Matt will wash the **dirty** dishes. _____

5. Joseph washed the **car** on Saturday. _____

6. The waterfall crashed **over** the cliff. _____

7. What will you give **her**? _____

8. The car **rolled** to a stop. _____

9. He **slowly** finished his homework. _____

10. My **nephew** will be 12 years old on Sunday. _____

11. The news program discussed the **war**. _____

12. Our **family** portrait was taken in the gazebo. _____

13. I **would like** to learn to fly a plane. _____

14. **My** hair needs to be trimmed. _____

15. **Strawberry** jam is her favorite. _____

16. The horse **quickly** galloped across the field. _____

17. **What** will you do next? _____

18. Please stand **and** introduce yourself. _____

19. My neighbor takes **great** pride in her garden. _____

20. She sang **well** tonight. _____

21. My grandmother is from **Trinidad**. _____

© 1999 American Education Publishing Co.

Cumulative Review

Directions: Write sentences containing the items listed.

1. Appositive _____

_____

2. Compound subject _____

_____

3. Antecedent and pronoun _____

_____

4. Correct use of the word **well** _____

_____

5. Commas for words in a series _____

_____

6. Direct address _____

_____

7. Compound predicate _____

_____

8. Singular possessive _____

_____

9. Plural possessive _____

_____

10. Compound sentence _____

_____

11. Correct use of quotation marks _____

_____

12. Correct use of the word **effect** _____

_____

Name: _____

Crossword Puzzle

Directions: Complete the crossword puzzle by using the clues.

ACROSS:

4. A _____ uses the words **like** or **as** to make a comparison.

5. _____ modify verbs.

6. An _____ tells to whom or for whom the action is performed.

10. The _____ of the sentence is the person, place, thing or idea the sentence is about.

11. Pairs of words which show relationships between words are called _____ .

12. Words that have opposite meanings are called _____ .

13. Words that have similar meanings are called _____ .

DOWN:

1. An _____ is a phrase which provides more information about a previous noun.

2. The _____ of the sentence is a verb that tells what the subject is doing.

3. A _____ answers what or whom after the verb.

7. Words that describe nouns are called _____ .

8. _____ compare two things by saying one is another.

9. _____ take the place of nouns.

Glossary

Adjective: A word that describes a noun.

Adverb: A word that tells when, where or how an action occurred.

Analogy: An analogy shows similarities, or things in common, between a pair of words.

Antecedent: The noun or nouns a pronoun refers to.

Antonyms: Words that have opposite meanings.

Appositive: A noun or pronoun placed after another noun or pronoun to further identify it.

Complete Sentence: A sentence that has both a simple subject and a simple predicate.

Conjunction: A joining word that connects two or more words or groups of words.

Contraction: A shortened form of two words. An apostrophe (') is used to show where some letters have been left out.

Dangling Modifier: A word or group of words that does not modify what it is supposed to modify.

Diamanté: A seven-line poem in the shape of a diamond.

Direct Object: A noun or pronoun which answers what or whom after the verb.

Faulty Parallelism: When parts of a sentence do not match grammatically or structurally.

Haiku: A Japanese verse of three lines having five, seven and five syllables each.

Independent Clause: Part of a sentence that contains a complete idea and can stand alone.

Indirect Object: A noun or pronoun that tells to whom or what or for whom or what the action is performed.

Interrogative Pronoun: A pronoun used to ask a question. **Who, what** and **which** are interrogative pronouns.

Irregular Verb: A verb whose past tense is not formed by adding **ed**.

Metaphor: A type of comparison that says one thing is another.

Noun: A word that names a person, place, thing or idea.

Object of a Preposition: The noun or pronoun that follows a preposition and adds to its meaning.

Parallel: Parts of a sentence which match grammatically and structurally.

Personal Pronoun: A word that takes the place of a noun. It refers to a person or a thing.

Possessive Pronoun: A pronoun that shows ownership.

Prefix: A syllable added to the beginning of a word that changes its meaning.

Preposition: A word that comes before a noun or pronoun and shows the relationship of that noun or pronoun to some other word in the sentence.

Prepositional Phrase: A group of words that includes a preposition, the object of the preposition and all modifiers.

Pronoun: A word that takes the place of a noun.

Root Word: The common stem that gives related words their basic meanings.

Run-On Sentence: Two or more sentences joined together without punctuation or a joining word.

Simile: A phrase that uses **like** or **as** to compare two things that are not alike.

Simple Predicate: A verb in a sentence that tells what the subject does, is doing, did or will do.

Simple Subject: A noun or pronoun that tells who or what the sentence is about.

Suffix: A syllable added to the end of a word that changes its meaning.

Synonyms: Words that have the same or almost the same meaning.

Tense: The way a verb is used to express time.

Verb: A word in a sentence that tells what something does or that something exists.

Answer Keys

Nouns

A **noun** names a person, place, thing or idea. There are several types of nouns.

Examples:
proper nouns: Joe, Jefferson Memorial
common nouns: dog, town
concrete nouns: book, stove
abstract nouns: fear, devotion
collective nouns: audience, flock

A word can be more than one type of noun.

Example: Dog is both a common and a concrete noun.

Directions: Write the type or types of each noun on the lines.

1. desk — common, concrete
2. ocean — common, concrete
3. love — common, abstract
4. cat — common, concrete
5. herd — common, concrete, collective
6. compassion — common, abstract
7. reputation — common, abstract
8. eyes — common, concrete
9. staff — common, concrete, collective
10. day — common, concrete
11. Roosevelt Building — proper, concrete
12. Mr. Timken — proper, concrete
13. life — common, abstract
14. porch — common, concrete
15. United States — proper, concrete or abstract

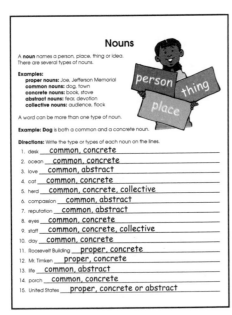

3

Verbs

A **verb** is a word that tells what something does or that something exists.

There are two types of verbs: **action** and **state of being**.

Examples:
Action: run, read
State of being: feel, sound, taste, stay, look, appear, grow, seem, smell and forms of **be**

Directions: Write **A** if the verb shows action. Write **S** if it shows state of being.

1. A — He helped his friend.
2. S — They appear happy and content.
3. A — Jordi drives to school each day.
4. A — The snowfall closed schools everywhere.
5. A — The dog sniffed at its food.
6. S — The meat tastes funny.
7. A — Did you taste the ice cream?
8. A — The young boy smelled the flowers.
9. S — She looked depressed.
10. A — The coach announced the dates of the scrimmage.
11. A — The owner of the store stocks all types of soda.
12. A — He dribbled the ball down the court.
13. S — "Everything seems to be in order," said the train conductor.

4

Nouns and Verbs

Some words can be used as both nouns and verbs.

Example:
The **bait** on his hook was a worm.
He couldn't **bait** his hook.

In the first sentence, **bait** is used as a **noun** because it names a thing. In the second sentence, **bait** is used as a **verb** because it shows action.

Directions: Write **noun** or **verb** for the word in bold in each sentence. The first one has been done for you.

verb — 1. She **piloted** the small plane across the Pacific Ocean.
verb — 2. Does she **water** her garden every night?
verb — 3. Did you **rebel** against the rules?
noun — 4. Dad will pound the fence **post** into the ground.
noun — 5. That was good **thinking**.
verb — 6. I **object** to your language!
noun — 7. He planned to become a **pilot** after graduation.
verb — 8. The teacher will **post** the new school calendar.
verb — 9. She was **thinking** of a donut.
noun — 10. The **object** of the search was forgotten.
noun — 11. She was a **rebel** in high school.
noun — 12. Would you like fresh **water** for your tea?

BAIT!

5

Simple Subjects

The **simple subject** of a sentence tells who or what the sentence is about. It is a noun or a pronoun.

Example: My **mom** is turning forty this year.
Mom is the simple subject.

Directions: Circle the simple subject in each sentence.

1. The (cat) ate all its food.
2. (They) watched the basketball game.
3. (Loretta) is going to lunch with her friend.
4. (Jose) likes strawberry jam on his toast.
5. The (reporter) interviewed the victim.
6. (She) turned down the volume.
7. The farm (animals) waited to be fed.
8. Can (you) lift weights?
9. The (fan) did little to cool the hot room.
10. (Thomas Jefferson) was one of the founding fathers of our country.
11. (I) have a lot to do tonight.
12. Will (you) go to the movie with us?
13. (We) enjoyed the day at the park.
14. Our (pet) is a dog.
15. (She) retrieved her homework from the garbage.

6

Personal Pronouns

Personal pronouns take the place of nouns. They refer to people or things. **I, me, we, she, he, him, her, you, they, them, us** and **it** are personal pronouns.

Directions: Circle the personal pronouns in each sentence.

1. (He) is a terrific friend.
2. Would (you) open the door?
3. Jim and (I) will arrive at ten o'clock.
4. Can (you) pick (me) up at the mall after dinner?
5. What did (you) do yesterday?
6. (They) are watching the game on television.
7. Jessie's mom took (us) to the movies.
8. (She) writes novels.
9. (They) gave (us) the refrigerator.
10. Is this the answer (she) intended to give?
11. What is (it)?
12. The dog yelped when (it) saw the cat.
13. (I) admire (him).
14. (We) parked the bikes by the tree.
15. The ants kept (us) from enjoying our picnic.
16. James gives (his) dog a bath once a week.

I, me, you. We! Him, her, them.

7

Possessive Pronouns

Possessive pronouns show ownership. **My, mine, your, yours, his, her, hers, their, theirs, our, ours** and **its** are possessive pronouns.

Directions: Circle the possessive pronouns in each sentence.

1. (My) dogs chase cats continually.
2. Jodi put (her) sunglasses on the dashboard.
3. (His) mother and (mine) are the same age.
4. The cat licked (its) paw.
5. (Their) anniversary is February 1.
6. This necklace is (yours).
7. We will carry (our) luggage into the airport.
8. (Our) parents took us to dinner.
9. (My) brother broke (his) leg.
10. (Her) report card was excellent.
11. Raspberry jam is (my) favorite.
12. Watch (your) step!
13. The house on the left is (mine).
14. (My) phone number is unlisted.
15. (Our) garden is growing out of control.
16. (Our) pumpkins are ten times larger than (theirs).

Mine!

8

© 1999 American Education Publishing Co.

108

Interrogative Pronouns

An **interrogative pronoun** asks a question. There are three interrogative pronouns: **who**, **what** and **which**.

Use **who** when speaking of persons.
Use **what** when speaking of things.
Use **which** when speaking of persons or things.

Examples:
Who will go? **What** will you do? **Which** of these is yours?

Who becomes **whom** when it is a direct object or an object of a preposition. The possessive form of **whom** is **whose**.

Examples:
To **whom** will you write?
Whose computer is that?

Directions: Write the correct interrogative pronoun.

1. __Whose__ wet raincoat is this?
2. __Who__ is the president of the United States?
3. __What__ is your name?
4. __Whose__ dog made this muddy mess?
5. __Whose__ cat ran away?
6. __Which__ of you is the culprit?
7. __What__ was your grade on the last test?
8. To __whom__ did you report?
9. __Whom__ do you believe now?
10. __Who__ is the leader of this English study group?

9

Personal and Possessive Pronouns

Directions: Write personal or possessive pronouns in the blanks to take the place of the words in bold. The first one has been done for you.

They	him	1. **Maisie and Marni** told **Trent** they would see him later.
He	them	2. **Spencer** told **Nancee and Sandi** good-bye.
It	his	3. **The bike** was parked near **Aaron's** house.
	They	4. **Maria, Matt and Greg** claimed the car was new.
	theirs	5. The dishes were **the property of Cindy and Jake**.
	hers	6. Is this **Carole's**?
He	their	7. **Jon** walked near **Jessica and Esau's** house.
	It	8. **The dog** barked all night long!
She	her	9. **Dawn** fell and hurt **Dawn's** knee.
They	its	10. **Cory and Devan** gave the dog **the dog's** dinner.
We	them	11. **Tori and I** gave **Brett and Reggie** a ride home.
	they	12. Do **Josh and Andrea** like cats?
They	us	13. **Sasha and Keesha** gave **Josh and me** a ride home.
	hers	14. Is this sweater **Marni's**?
	it	15. The cat meowed because **the cat** was hungry.

10

Pronoun/Antecedent Agreement

Often, a **pronoun** is used in place of a noun to avoid repeating the noun again in the same sentence. The noun that a pronoun refers to is called its **antecedent**. The word "antecedent" means "going before."

If the noun is singular, the pronoun that takes its place must also be singular. If the noun is plural, the pronoun that takes its place must also be plural. This is called *agreement* between the pronoun and its antecedent.

Examples:
Mary (singular noun) said **she** (singular pronoun) would dance.
The **dogs** (plural noun) took **their** (plural pronoun) dishes outside.

When the noun is singular and the gender unknown, it is correct to use either "his" or "his or her."

Directions: Rewrite the sentences so the pronouns and nouns agree. The first one has been done for you.

1. Every student opened their book.
   Every student opened his book.
   Also correct: Every student opened his or her book.
2. Has anyone lost their wallet lately?
   Has anyone lost his or her wallet lately?
3. Somebody found the wallet under their desk.
   Somebody found the wallet under his desk.
4. Someone will have to file their report.
   Someone will have to file his or her report.
5. Every dog has their day!
   Every dog has its day!
6. I felt Ted had mine best interests at heart.
   I felt Ted had my best interests at heart.

11

Pronoun/Antecedent Agreement

Directions: Write a pronoun that agrees with the antecedent.

1. Donald said __he__ would go to the store.
2. My friend discovered __his (or her)__ wallet had been stolen.
3. The cat licked __its__ paw.
4. Did any woman here lose __her__ necklace?
5. Someone will have to give __his (or her)__ report.
6. Jennifer wished __she__ had not come.
7. All the children decided __they__ would attend.
8. My grandmother hurt __her__ back while gardening.
9. Jerry, Marco and I hope __we__ win the game.
10. Sandra looked for __her__ missing homework.
11. The family had __its__ celebration.
12. My dog jumps out of __its__ pen.
13. Somebody needs to remove __his (or her)__ clothes from this chair.
14. Everything has __its__ place in Grandma's house.
15. The team will receive __their__ uniforms on Monday.
16. Each artist wants __his (or her)__ painting to win the prize.

12

Appositives

An **appositive** is a noun or pronoun placed after another noun or pronoun to further identify or rename it. An appositive and the words that go with it are usually set off from the rest of the sentence with commas. Commas are not used if the appositive tells "which one."

Example: Angela's mother, **Ms. Glover**, will visit our school.

Commas are needed because **Ms. Glover** renames Angela's mother.

Example: Angela's neighbor Joan will visit our school.

Commas are not needed because the appositive "Joan" tells **which** neighbor.

Directions: Write the appositive in each sentence in the blank. The first one has been done for you.

1. Tina — My friend Tina wants a horse.
2. Horses — She subscribes to the magazine *Horses*.
3. "Brownie" — Her horse is the gelding "Brownie."
4. convertible — We rode in her new car, a convertible.
5. bracelet — Her gift was jewelry, a bracelet.
6. senator — Have you met Ms. Abbott, the senator?
7. Karl — My cousin Karl is very shy.
8. Oaties — Do you eat the cereal Oaties?
9. Samantha — Kiki's cat, Samantha, will eat only tuna.
10. Jones — My last name, Jones, is very common.

13

Verb Tense

Tense is the way a verb is used to express time. To explain what is happening right now, use the **present tense**.

Example: He **is** singing well. He **sings** well.

To explain what has already happened, use the **past tense**.

Example: He **sang** well.

To explain what will happen, use the **future tense**.

Example: He **will sing** well.

Directions: Rewrite each sentence so the verbs are in the same tense. The first one has been done for you.

1. He ran, he jumped, then he is flying.
   He ran, he jumped, then he flew.
2. He was crying, then he will stop.
   He was crying, then he stopped.
3. She feels happy, but she was not sure why.
   She feels happy, but she is not sure why.
4. He is my friend, so was she.
   He is my friend, and so is she.
5. She bit into the cake and says it is good.
   She bit into the cake and said it was good.
6. He laughs first and then told us the joke.
   He laughed first, then told us the joke.

14

Verb Tense

Directions: Write a sentence using the present tense of each verb.

1. walk _____

2. dream _____

3. achieve _____
_____

Answers will vary.

4. dance _____

5. study _____

6. hike _____

Directions: Write a sentence using the future tense of each verb.

7. bake _____

8. write _____

9. talk _____

15

Verb Tense

Verbs can be **present**, **past** or **past participle**.

Add **d** or **ed** to form the past tense.

Past-participle verbs also use a helping verb such as **has** or **have**.

Examples:

Present	Past	Past Participle
help	helped	has or have helped
skip	skipped	has or have skipped

Directions: Write the past and past-participle forms of each present tense verb.

Present	Past	Past Participle
1. paint	painted	has (have) painted
2. dream	dreamed	has (have) dreamed
3. play	played	has (have) played
4. approach	approached	has (have) approached
5. hop	hopped	has (have) hopped
6. climb	climbed	has (have) climbed
7. dance	danced	has (have) danced
8. appear	appeared	has (have) appeared
9. watch	watched	has (have) watched
10. dive	dove, dived	has (have) dived
11. hurry	hurried	has (have) hurried
12. discover	discovered	has (have) discovered
13. decorate	decorated	has (have) decorated
14. close	closed	has (have) closed
15. jump	jumped	has (have) jumped

16

Irregular Verb Forms

The past tense of most verbs is formed by adding **ed**. Verbs that do not follow this format are called **irregular verbs**.

The irregular verb chart shows a few of the many verbs with irregular forms.

Irregular Verb Chart		
Present Tense	**Past Tense**	**Past Participle**
go	went	has, have or had gone
do	did	has, have or had done
fly	flew	has, have or had flown
grow	grew	has, have or had grown
ride	rode	has, have or had ridden
see	saw	has, have or had seen
sing	sang	has, have or had sung
swim	swam	has, have or had swum
throw	threw	has, have or had thrown

The words **have** and **has** can be separated from the irregular verb by other words in the sentence.

Directions: Choose the correct verb form from the chart to complete the sentences. The first one has been done for you.

1. The pilot had never before **flown** that type of plane.

2. She put on her bathing suit and **swam** 2 miles.

3. The tall boy had **grown** 2 inches over the summer.

4. She insisted she had **done** her homework.

5. He **saw** them walking down the street.

6. She **rode** the horse around the track.

7. The pitcher has **thrown** the ball many times.

8. He can **swim** safely in the deepest water.

17

Irregular Verb Forms

Directions: Use the irregular verb chart on the previous page. Write the correct verb form to complete each sentence.

1. Has she ever **grown** carrots in her garden?

2. She was so angry she **threw** a tantrum.

3. The bird had sometimes **flown** from its cage.

4. The cowboy has never **ridden** that horse before.

5. Will you **go** to the store with me?

6. He said he had often **seen** her walking on his street.

7. She insisted she has not **grown** taller this year.

8. He **swam** briskly across the pool.

9. Have the insects **flown** away?

10. Has anyone **seen** my sister lately?

11. He hasn't **done** the dishes once this week!

12. Has she been **thrown** out of the game for cheating?

13. I haven't **seen** her yet today.

14. The airplane **flew** slowly by the airport.

15. Have you **ridden** your bike yet this week?

18

Simple Predicates

The **simple predicate** of a sentence tells what the subject does, is doing, did or will do. The simple predicate is always a verb.

Example:
My mom **is turning** forty this year.
"Is turning" is the simple predicate.

Directions: Underline the simple predicate in each sentence. Include all helping verbs.

1. I bought school supplies at the mall.

2. The tiger chased its prey.

3. Mark will be arriving shortly.

4. The hamburgers are cooking now.

5. We will attend my sister's wedding.

6. The dental hygienist cleaned my teeth.

7. My socks are hanging on the clothesline.

8. Where are you going?

9. The dog is running toward its owner.

10. Ramos watched the tornado in fear.

11. Please wash the dishes after dinner.

12. My dad cleaned the garage yesterday.

13. We are going hiking at Yellowstone today.

14. The picture shows our entire family at the family picnic.

15. Our coach will give us a pep talk before the game.

19

Parallel Structure

Parts of a sentence are **parallel** when they "match" grammatically and structurally.

Faulty parallelism occurs when the parts of a sentence do not match grammatically and structurally.

For sentences to be parallel, all parts of a sentence—including the verbs, nouns and phrases—must match. This means that, in most cases, verbs should be in the same tense.

Examples:
Correct: She liked running, jumping and swinging outdoors.
Incorrect: She liked running, jumping and to swing outdoors.

In the correct sentence, all three of the actions the girl liked to do end in **ing**. In the incorrect sentence, they do not.

Directions: Rewrite the sentences so all elements are parallel. The first one has been done for you.

1. Politicians like making speeches and also to shake hands.
   Politicians like making speeches and shaking hands.

2. He liked singing, acting and to perform in general.
   He liked singing, acting and performing in general.

3. The cake had icing, sprinkles and also has small candy hearts.
   The cake had icing, sprinkles and small candy hearts.

4. The drink was cold, frosty and also is a thirst-quencher.
   The drink was cold, frosty and a thirst-quencher.

5. She was asking when we would arrive, and I told her.
   She asked when we would arrive, and I told her.

6. Liz felt like shouting, singing and to jump.
   Liz felt like shouting, singing and jumping.

20

Subject/Verb Agreement

Singular subjects require singular verbs. **Plural subjects** require plural verbs. The subject and verb must agree in a sentence.

Example:
Singular: My dog runs across the field.
Plural: My dogs run across the field.

Directions: Circle the correct verb in each sentence.

1. Maria (talk/talks) to me each day at lunch.
2. Mom, Dad and I (is/are) going to the park to play catch.
3. Mr. and Mrs. Ramirez (dance/dances) well together.
4. Astronauts (hope/hopes) for a successful shuttle mission.
5. Trees (prevent/prevents) erosion.
6. The student (is/are) late.
7. She (ask/asks) for directions to the senior high gym.
8. The elephants (plod/plods) across the grassland to the watering hole.
9. My friend's name (is/are) Rebecca.
10. Many people (enjoy/enjoys) orchestra concerts.
11. The pencils (is/are) sharpened.
12. My backpack (hold/holds) a lot of things.
13. The wind (blow/blows) to the south.
14. Sam (collect/collects) butterflies.
15. They (love/loves) cotton candy.

The SINGULAR SUBJECT

21

Dangling Modifiers

A **dangling modifier** is a word or group of words that does not modify what it is supposed to modify. To correct dangling modifiers, supply the missing words to which the modifiers refer.

Examples:
Incorrect: While doing the laundry, the dog barked.
Correct: While I was doing the laundry, the dog barked.

In the **incorrect** sentence, it sounds as though the dog is doing the laundry. In the **correct** sentence, it's clear that **I** is the subject of the sentence.

Directions: Rewrite the sentences to make the subject of the sentence clear and eliminate dangling modifiers. The first one has been done for you.

1. While eating our hot dogs, the doctor called.
   While we were eating our hot dogs, the doctor called.
2. Living in Cincinnati, the ball park is nearby.
   I live in Cincinnati, and the ball park is nearby.
3. While watching the movie, the TV screen went blank.
   While we were watching the movie, the TV screen went blank.
4. While listening to the concert, the lights went out.
   While we were listening to the concert, the lights went out.
5. Tossed regularly, anyone can make great salad.
   Anyone can make a great salad if it's tossed regularly.
6. The programmer saw something on his screen that surprised him.
   The programmer saw something that surprised him on the screen.

MODIFIERS

22

Review

Directions: Rewrite the sentences to correct the faulty parallels.

1. The cookies were sweet, crunchy and are delicious.
   The cookies were sweet, crunchy and delicious.
2. The town was barren, windswept and is empty.
   The town was barren, windswept and empty.
3. The dog was black, long-haired and is quite friendly.
   The dog was black, long-haired and quite friendly.
4. My favorite dinners are macaroni and cheese, spaghetti and I loved fish.
   My favorite dinners are macaroni and cheese, spaghetti and fish.

Directions: Rewrite the sentences to make the verb tenses consistent.

5. We laughed, cried and were jumping for joy.
   We laughed, cried and jumped for joy.
6. She sang, danced and was doing somersaults.
   She sang, danced and did somersaults.
7. The class researched, studied and were writing their reports.
   The class researched, studied and wrote their reports.
8. Bob and Sue talked about their vacation and share their experiences.
   Bob and Sue talked about their vacation and shared their experiences.

Directions: Circle the pronouns that agree with their antecedents.

9. She left (her/their) purse at the dance.
10. Each dog wagged (its/their) tail.
11. We walked to (our/my) car.
12. The lion watched (his/its) prey.

23

Review   Answers may vary.

Directions: Rewrite the sentences to correct the dangling modifiers.

1. Living nearby, the office was convenient for her.
   She lived nearby and the office was convenient for her.
2. While doing my homework, the doorbell rang.
   While I was doing my homework, the doorbell rang.
3. Watching over her shoulder, she hurried away.
   She watched over her shoulder and hurried away.
4. Drinking from the large mug, he choked.
   While he was drinking from the large mug, he choked.

Directions: Circle the correct pronouns.

5. She laughed at my brother and (I/me).
6. At dawn, (he and I/him and me) were still talking.
7. Someone left (his or her/their) coat on the floor.
8. Lauren said (her/she) would not be late.

Directions: Circle the appositive.

9. The school nurse, (Ms. Franklin) was worried about him.
10. The car, (a Volkswagen) was illegally parked.
11. My hero, (Babe Ruth) was an outstanding baseball player.
12. Is that car, (the plum-colored one) for sale?
13. Will Mr. Zimmer, (Todd's father) buy that car?

REVIEW
NOUNS VERBS
SIMPLE SUBJECTS
PERSONAL PRONOUNS
POSSESSIVE PRONOUNS
INTERROGATIVE PRONOUNS
ANTECEDENTS
APPOSITIVES
SIMPLE PREDICATES

24

Adjectives

Adjectives describe nouns.

Examples:
tall girl
soft voice
clean hands

Directions: Circle the adjectives. Underline the nouns they describe. Some sentences may have more than one set of adjectives and nouns.

1. The (lonely) man sat in the (dilapidated) house.
2. I hope the (large) crop of grapes will soon ripen.
3. The (white) boxes house honeybees.
4. (My) (rambunctious) puppy knocked over the (valuable) (flower) vase.
5. The (unsinkable) Titanic sank after striking a (gigantic) iceberg.
6. His grades showed (his) (tremendous) effort.
7. There are (many) (purple) flowers in the (large) arrangement.
8. (These) (sweet) peaches are the (best) I've tasted.
9. The newsletter describes (several) (educational) workshops.
10. The rodeo featured (professional) riders and (funny) clowns.
11. (My) (evening) pottery class is (full) of (very) (interesting) people.
12. (My) (older) brother loves (his) (new) pickup truck.
13. (Tami's) family bought a (big-screen) TV.

25

Adverbs

Adverbs tell when, where or how an action occurred.

When? Where? How?

Examples:
I'll go **tomorrow**. (when)
I sleep **upstairs**. (where)
I screamed **loudly**. (how)

Directions: Circle the adverb and underline the verb it modifies. Write the question (when, where or how) the adverb answers.

1. I ran (quickly) toward the finish line.   how
2. (Today) we will receive our report cards.   when
3. He swam (smoothly) through the pool.   how
4. Many explorers searched (endlessly) for new lands.   how
5. He looked (up) into the sky.   where
6. My friend drove (away) in her new car.   where
7. (Later) we will search for your missing wallet.   when
8. Most kings rule their kingdoms (regally).   how
9. New plants must be watered (daily).   when
10. The stream near our house is (heavily) polluted.   how
11. My brother likes to dive (backward) into our pool.   how

26

Adjectives and Adverbs

Directions: Write **adjective** or **adverb** in the blanks to describe the words in bold. The first one has been done for you.

adjective   1. Her **old** boots were caked with mud.

adjective   2. The baby was **cranky**.

adverb   3. He took the test **yesterday**.

adjective   4. I heard the **funniest** story last week!

adverb   5. She left her wet shoes **outside**.

adjective   6. Isn't that the **fluffiest** cat you've ever seen?

adverb   7. He ran **around** the track twice.

adjective   8. Our elderly neighbor lady seems **lonely**.

adjective   9. His **kind** smile lifted my dragging spirits.

adverb   10. **Someday** I'll meet the friend of my dreams!

adverb   11. His cat never meows **indoors**.

adverb   12. Carlos hung his new shirts **back** in the closet.

adverb   13. Put that valuable vase **down** immediately!

adjective   14. She is the most **joyful** child!

adjective   15. Jonathan's wool sweater is totally **moth-eaten**.

27

Adjectives: Positive, Comparative and Superlative

There are three degrees of comparison adjectives: **positive, comparative** and **superlative**. The **positive degree** is the adjective itself. The **comparative** and **superlative** degrees are formed by adding **er** and **est**, respectively, to most one-syllable adjectives. The form of the word changes when the adjective is irregular, for example, **good, better, best**.

Most adjectives of two or more syllables require the words "more" or "most" to form the comparative and superlative degrees.

Examples:
Positive:	big	eager
Comparative:	bigger	more eager
Superlative:	biggest	most eager

Directions: Write the positive, comparative or superlative forms of these adjectives.

Positive	Comparative	Superlative
1. hard	harder	hardest
2. happy	happier	happiest
3. difficult	more difficult	most difficult
4. cold	colder	coldest
5. easy	easier	easiest
6. large	larger	largest
7. little	less	least
8. shiny	shinier	shiniest
9. round	rounder	roundest
10. beautiful	more beautiful	most beautiful

28

Adverbs: Positive, Comparative and Superlative

There are also three degrees of comparison adverbs: **positive, comparative** and **superlative**. They follow the same rules as adjectives.

Example:
Positive:	rapidly	far
Comparative:	more rapidly	farther
Superlative:	most rapidly	farthest

Directions: Write the positive, comparative or superlative forms of these adverbs.

Positive	Comparative	Superlative
1. easily	more easily	most easily
2. quickly	more quickly	most quickly
3. hopefully	more hopefully	most hopefully
4. bravely	more bravely	most bravely
5. strongly	more strongly	most strongly
6. near	nearer	nearest
7. cleverly	more cleverly	most cleverly
8. gracefully	more gracefully	most gracefully
9. humbly	more humbly	most humbly
10. excitedly	more excitedly	most excitedly
11. handsomely	more handsomely	most handsomely
12. slowly	more slowly	most slowly

29

Prepositions

A **preposition** is a word that comes before a noun or pronoun and shows the relationship of that noun or pronoun to some other word in the sentence.

The **object of a preposition** is the noun or pronoun that follows a preposition and adds to its meaning.

A **prepositional phrase** includes the preposition, the object of the preposition and all modifiers.

Example:
She gave him a pat **on his back**.
On is the preposition.
Back is the object of the preposition.
His is a possessive pronoun.

Common Prepositions
about	down	near	through
above	for	of	to
across	from	off	up
at	in	on	with
behind	into	out	within
by	like	past	without

Directions: Underline the prepositional phrases. Circle the prepositions. Some sentences have more than one prepositional phrase. The first one has been done for you.

1. He claimed he felt (at) home only (on) the West Coast.
2. She went (up) the street, then (down) the block.
3. The famous poet was (near) death.
4. The beautiful birthday card was (from) her father.
5. He left his wallet (at) home.
6. Her speech was totally (without) humor and boring as well.
7. I think he's (from) New York City.
8. Kari wanted (to) go (with) her mother (to) the mall.

30

Prepositions

Directions: Complete the sentences by writing objects for the prepositions. The first one has been done for you.

1. He was standing at the corner of Fifth and Main.

2. She saw her friend across _____

3. Have you ever looked beyond _____

4. His contact lens fell into _____

5. Have _____

6. She _____

7. Is that _____

8. She was daydreaming and walked past _____

9. The book was hidden behind _____

10. The young couple had fallen in _____

11. She insisted she was through _____

12. He sat down near _____

13. She forgot her umbrella at _____

14. Have you ever thought of _____

15. Henry found his glasses on _____

Answers will vary.

31

Object of a Preposition

The **object of a preposition** is the noun or pronoun that follows the preposition and adds to its meaning.

Example:
Correct: Devan smiled at (preposition) **Tori** (noun: object of the preposition) and **me** (pronoun: object of the same preposition.)
Correct: Devan smiled at Tori. Devan smiled at me. Devan smiled at Tori and me.
Incorrect: Devan smiled at Tori and I.

Tip: If you are unsure of the correct pronoun to use, pair each pronoun with the verb and say the phrase out loud to find out which pronoun is correct.

Directions: Write the correct pronouns on the blanks. The first one has been done for you.

him   1. It sounded like a good idea to Sue and (he/him).

her   2. I asked Abby if I could attend with (her/she).

us   3. To (we/us), holidays are very important.

us   4. Between (we/us), we finished the job quickly.

him and me   5. They gave the award to (he and I/him and me).

me   6. The party was for my brother and (I/me).

his   7. I studied at (his/him) house.

their   8. Tanya and the others arrived late in spite of (they/their) fast car.

we   9. After (we/us) went to the zoo, we stopped at the museum.

his   10. The chips are in the bag on top of (his/him) refrigerator.

32

Direct Objects

A **direct object** is a noun or pronoun. It answers the question **who** or **what** after a verb.

Examples:
My mom baked **bread**.
Bread is the direct object. It tells **what** Mom baked.
We saw **Steve**.
Steve is the direct object. It tells **who** we saw.

Directions: Write a direct object in each sentence.

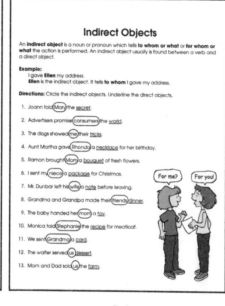

1. My dog likes _____. WHAT?
2. My favorite drink is _____. WHAT?
3. I saw _____.
4. _____
5. _____ through the room. WHAT?
6. I packed a _____ for lunch. WHAT?
7. We watched _____ play basketball. WHOM?
8. I finished my _____. WHAT?
9. The artist sketched the _____. WHAT?
10. He greets _____ at the door. WHOM?
11. The team attended the victory _____. WHAT?
12. The beautician cut my _____. WHAT?
13. Tamika will write _____. WHAT?

Answers will vary.

33

Indirect Objects

An **indirect object** is a noun or pronoun which tells **to whom or what** or **for whom or what** the action is performed. An indirect object usually is found between a verb and a direct object.

Example:
I gave **Ellen** my address.
Ellen is the indirect object. It tells **to whom** I gave my address.

Directions: Circle the indirect objects. Underline the direct objects.

1. Joann told (Mary) the secret.
2. Advertisers promise (consumers) the world.
3. The dogs showed (me) their tricks.
4. Aunt Martha gave (Rhonda) a necklace for her birthday.
5. Ramon brought (Mom) a bouquet of fresh flowers.
6. I sent my (niece) a package for Christmas.
7. Mr. Dunbar left his (wife) a note before leaving.
8. Grandma and Grandpa made their (friends) dinner.
9. The baby handed her (mom) a toy.
10. Monica told (Stephanie) the recipe for meatloaf.
11. We sent (Grandma) a card.
12. The waiter served (us) dessert.
13. Mom and Dad sold (us) the farm.

For me? For you!

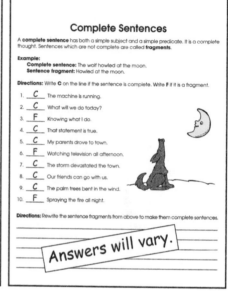

34

Complete Sentences

A **complete sentence** has both a simple subject and a simple predicate. It is a complete thought. Sentences which are not complete are called **fragments**.

Example:
Complete sentence: The wolf howled at the moon.
Sentence fragment: Howled at the moon.

Directions: Write **C** on the line if the sentence is complete. Write **F** if it is a fragment.

1. _C_ The machine is running.
2. _C_ What will we do today?
3. _F_ Knowing what I do.
4. _C_ That statement is true.
5. _C_ My parents drove to town.
6. _F_ Watching television all afternoon.
7. _C_ The storm devastated the town.
8. _C_ Our friends can go with us.
9. _C_ The palm trees bent in the wind.
10. _F_ Spraying the fire all night.

Directions: Rewrite the sentence fragments from above to make them complete sentences.

_____

Answers will vary.

35

Run-On Sentences

A **run-on sentence** occurs when two or more sentences are joined together without punctuation or a joining word. Run-on sentences should be divided into two or more separate sentences.

Example:
Run-on sentence: My parents, sister, brother and I went to the park we saw many animals we had fun.
Correct: My parents, sister, brother and I went to the park. We saw many animals and had fun.

Directions: Rewrite the run-on sentences correctly. Sample answers:

1. The dog energetically chased the ball I kept throwing him the ball for a half hour.
   The dog energetically chased the ball. I kept throwing him the ball for a half hour.

2. The restaurant served scrambled eggs and bacon for breakfast I had some and they were delicious.
   The restaurant served bacon and scrambled eggs for breakfast. I had some, and they were delicious.

3. The lightning struck close to our house it scared my little brother and my grandmother called to see if we were safe.
   The lightning struck close to our house. It scared my little brother. My grandmother called to see if we were safe.

36

Conjunctions

Conjunctions are joining words that connect two or more words or groups of words. The words **and, but, or, nor, so** and **because** are conjunctions.

Join two sentences with **and** when they are more or less equal.

Example: John will be there, **and** he will bring the punch.

Join two sentences with **but** when the second sentence contradicts the first.

Example: John will be there, **but** his brother will not.

Join two sentences with **or** or **nor** when they name a choice.

Example: John may bring punch, **or** he may bring soda.

Join two sentences with **because** or **so** when the second one names a reason for the first one.

Example: John will bring punch **because** he's on the refreshment committee.

Directions: Finish each sentence using the conjunction correctly. The first one has been done for you.

1. My best friend was absent, so _I ate lunch alone._
2. The test was easy, but _____
3. I wanted to go because _____
4. We did our homework _____
5. We _____
6. I felt _____
7. Josh _____
8. We worked quickly, and _____

Answers will vary.

37

Conjunctions

The conjunctions **and, or, but** and **nor** can be used to make a compound subject, a compound predicate or a compound sentence.

Me AND You

Examples:
Compound subject: My friend **and** I will go to the mall.
Compound predicate: We ran **and** jumped in gym class.
Compound sentence: I am a talented violinist, **but** my father is better.

Directions: Write two sentences of your own in each section.

Compound subject:
1. _____
2. _____

Compound predicate:
1. _____
2. _____

Compound sentence:
1. _____
2. _____

Answers will vary.

38

ENGLISH 6

Page 39

Review

Directions: Write the missing verb tenses.

Present	Past	Past Participle
1. catch	caught	has (have) caught
2. stir	stirred	has (have) stirred
3. bake	baked	has (have) baked
4. go	went	has (have) gone
5. say	said	has (have) said

Directions: Circle the simple subject and underline the simple predicate in each sentence.

6. Maria got sunburned at the beach.
7. The class watched the program.
8. The tomatoes are ripening.
9. We went grocery shopping.
10. The cross country team practiced all summer.

Directions: Write the missing adjective or adverb forms below.

Positive	Comparative	Superlative
11. friendly	more friendly	most friendly
12. small	smaller	smallest
13. fun	more fun	most fun
14. attractive	more attractive	most attractive

39

Page 40

Review

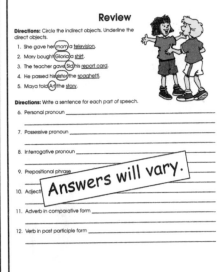

Directions: Circle the indirect objects. Underline the direct objects.

1. She gave her mom a television.
2. Mary bought Gloria a shirt.
3. The teacher gave Sid his report card.
4. He passed his sister the spaghetti.
5. Maya told Art the story.

Directions: Write a sentence for each part of speech.

6. Personal pronoun _____
7. Possessive pronoun _____
8. Interrogative pronoun _____
9. Prepositional phrase _____

Answers will vary.

10. Adjective _____
11. Adverb in comparative form _____
12. Verb in past participle form _____

40

Page 41

Review

Directions: Write **noun** or **verb** to describe the words in bold.

noun	1. She is one of the fastest **runners** I've seen.
verb	2. She is **running** very fast!
verb	3. She **thought** he was handsome.
noun	4. Please share your **thoughts** with me.
verb	5. I will **watch** the volleyball game on video.
noun	6. The sailor fell asleep during his **watch**.
noun	7. My grandmother believes my purchase was a real **find**.
verb	8. I hope to **find** my lost books.

Directions: Rewrite the verb in the correct tense.

swam	9. She **swim** across the lake in 2 hours.
ridden	10. He has **ride** horses for years.
seen	11. Have you **saw** my sister?
flew	12. We **fly** on an airplane last week.
instructed	13. My father had **instruct** me in the language.
drove	14. I **drive** to the store yesterday.
began	15. The movie **begin** late.
did	16. Where **do** you go yesterday?

Directions: Circle the pronouns.

17. She and I told them to forget it.
18. They all wondered if her dad would drive his new car.
19. We want our parents to believe us.
20. My picture was taken at her home.

41

Page 42

Review

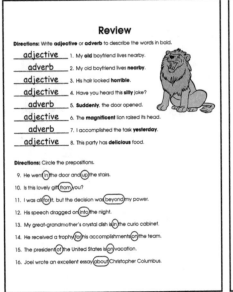

Directions: Write **adjective** or **adverb** to describe the words in bold.

adjective	1. My **old** boyfriend lives nearby.
adverb	2. My old boyfriend lives **nearby**.
adjective	3. His hair looked **horrible**.
adjective	4. Have you heard this **silly** joke?
adverb	5. **Suddenly**, the door opened.
adjective	6. The **magnificent** lion raised its head.
adverb	7. I accomplished the task **yesterday**.
adjective	8. This party has **delicious** food.

Directions: Circle the prepositions.

9. He went in the door and up the stairs.
10. Is this lovely gift from you?
11. I was all for it, but the decision was beyond my power.
12. His speech dragged on into the night.
13. My great-grandmother's crystal dish is in the curio cabinet.
14. He received a trophy for his accomplishments on the team.
15. The president of the United States is on vacation.
16. Joel wrote an excellent essay about Christopher Columbus.

42

Page 43

Commas

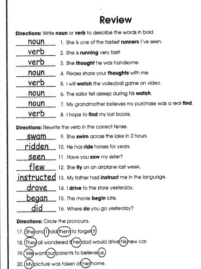

Use commas . . .
. . . after introductory phrases
. . . to set off nouns of direct address
. . . to set off appositives from the words that go with them
. . . to set off words that interrupt the flow of the sentence
. . . to separate words or groups of words in a series

Examples:
Introductory phrase: Of course, I'd be happy to attend.
Noun of direct address: Ms. Williams, please sit here.
To set off appositives: Lee, **the club president**, sat beside me.
Words interrupting flow: My cousin, **who's 13**, will also be there.
Words in a series: I ate **popcorn, peanuts, oats** and **barley**.
    or   I ate **popcorn, peanuts, oats,** and **barley**.

Note: The final comma is optional when punctuating words in a series.

Directions: Identify how the commas are used in each sentence.
Write: **I** for introductory phrase
N for noun of direct address
A for appositive
WF for words interrupting flow
WS for words in a series

I	1. Yes, she is my sister.
A	2. My teacher, Mr. Hopkins, is very fair.
WS	3. Her favorite fruits are oranges, plums and grapes.
A	4. The city mayor, Carla Ellison, is quite young.
WS	5. I will buy bread, milk, fruit and ice cream.
WF	6. Her crying, which was quite loud, soon gave me a headache.
N	7. Stephanie, please answer the question.
I	8. So, do you know her?
I	9. Unfortunately, the item is not returnable.
WS	10. My sister, my cousin and my friend will accompany me on vacation.
A	11. My grandparents, Rose and Bill, are both 57 years old.

43

Page 44

Commas

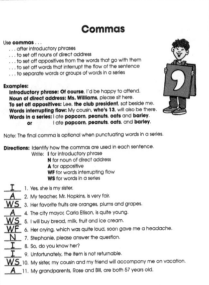

Commas are important, and you should know when to use them!

Directions: Use commas to punctuate these sentences correctly.

1. I'll visit her, however, not until I'm ready.
2. She ordered coats, gloves and a hat from the catalog.
3. Eun-Jung, the new girl, looked ill at ease.
4. Certainly, I'll show Eun-Jung around school.
5. Yes, I'll be glad to help her.
6. I paid, nevertheless, I was unhappy with the price.
7. I bought stamps, envelopes and plenty of postcards.
8. No, I told you I was not going.
9. The date, November 12, was not convenient.
10. Her earache, which kept her up all night, stopped at dawn.
11. My nephew, who loves bike riding, will go with us.
12. He'll bring hiking boots, a tent and food.
13. The cat, a Himalayan, was beautiful.
14. The tennis player, a professional in every sense, signed autographs.
15. No, you can't stay out past 10:00 P.M.

44

Semicolons

A **semicolon** (;) signals a reader to pause longer than for a comma, but not as long as for a period. Semicolons are used between closely related independent clauses not joined by **and**, **or**, **nor**, **for**, **yet** or **but**.

An **independent clause** contains a complete idea and can stand alone.

Example: Rena was outgoing; her sister was shy.

Directions: Use semicolons to punctuate these sentences correctly. Some sentences require more than one semicolon.

1. Jeff wanted coffee; Sally wanted milk.
2. I thought he was kind; she thought he was grouchy.
3. "I came; I saw; I conquered," wrote Julius Caesar.
4. Jessica read books; she also read magazines.
5. I wanted a new coat; my old one was too small.
6. The airport was fogged-in; the planes could not land.
7. Now, he regrets his comments; it's too late to retract them.
8. The girls were thrilled; their mothers were not.

Directions: Use a semicolon and an independent clause to complete the sentences.

9. She liked him _____
10. I chose a red shirt _____
11. Andrea sang well _____
12. She jumped _____
13. Dancing is _____
14. The man wa[s] _____
15. The fire looked flat _____
16. My bike is missing _____

Answers will vary.

45

Colons

Use a **colon** . . .
. . . after the salutation of a business letter
. . . between the hour and the minute when showing time
. . . between the volume and page number of a periodical
. . . between chapters and verses of the Bible
. . . before a list of three or more items
. . . to introduce a long statement or quotation

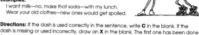

Dear Mr. Miller:

I would like to place an order for five of your 1 ton scales. Please contact me, concerning price and delivery date.

Sincerely,
Ms. Jones

Examples:
Salutation: Dear Madame:
Hour and minute: 8:45 P.M.
Periodical volume and page number: Newsweek 11:32
Bible chapter and verse: John 3:16
Before a list of three or more items: Buy these: fruit, cereal, cheese
To introduce a long statement or quotation: Author Willa Cather said this about experiencing life: "There are only two or three human stories, and they go on repeating themselves as fiercely as if they had never happened before."

Directions: Use colons to punctuate these sentences correctly. Some sentences require more than one colon.

1. At 12:45 the president said this: "Where's my lunch?"
2. Look in Proverbs 1:12 for the answer.
3. Don't forget to order these items: boots, socks, shoes and leggings.
4. Ask the librarian for *Weekly Reader* 3:14.
5. Dear Sir: Please send me two copies of your report.
6. Avoid these at all costs: bad jokes, bad company, bad manners.
7. The statement is in either Genesis 1:6 or Exodus 3:2.
8. At 9:15 P.M., she checked in, and at 6:45 A.M., she checked out.
9. I felt all these things at once: joy, anger and sadness.
10. Here's a phrase President Bush liked: "A thousand points of light."

46

Dashes

Dashes (—) are used to indicate sudden changes of thought.

Examples:
I want milk—no, make that soda—with my lunch.
Wear your old clothes—new ones would get spoiled.

Directions: If the dash is used correctly in the sentence, write **C** in the blank. If the dash is missing or used incorrectly, draw an **X** in the blank. The first one has been done for you.

C 1. No one—not even my dad—knows about the surprise.
X 2. Ask—him—no I will to come to the party.
X 3. I'll tell you the answer oh, the phone just rang!
C 4. Everyone thought—even her brother—that she looked pretty.
C 5. Can you please—oh, forget it!
X 6. Just stop it I really mean it!
C 7. Tell her that I'll—never mind—I'll tell her myself!
X 8. Everyone especially Anna is overwhelmed.
C 9. I wish everyone could—forgive me—I'm sorry!
C 10. The kids—all six of them—piled into the backseat.

Directions: Write two sentences of your own that include dashes.

11. _____
12. _____

Answers will vary.

47

Quotation Marks

Quotation marks are used to enclose a speaker's exact words. Use commas to set off a direct quotation from other words in the sentence.

Examples:
Kira smiled and said, "Quotation marks come in handy."
"Yes," Josh said, "I'll take two."

Directions: If quotation marks and commas are used correctly, write **C** in the blank. If they are used incorrectly, write an **X** in the blank. The first one has been done for you.

C 1. "I suppose," Elizabeth remarked, "that you'll be there on time."
X 2. "Please let me help! insisted Mark.
X 3. I'll be ready in 2 minutes!" her father said.
C 4. "Just breathe slowly." the nurse said, "and calm down."
X 5. "No one understands me" William whined.
C 6. "Would you like more milk?" Jasmine asked politely.
X 7. "No thanks, her grandpa replied. "I have plenty."
C 8. "What a beautiful morning!" Jessica yelled.
X 9. "Yes, it certainly is" her mother agreed.
C 10. "Whose purse is this?" asked Andrea.
X 11. It's mine" said Stephanie. "Thank you."
C 12. "Can you play the piano?" asked Heather.
X 13. "Music is my hobby," Jonathan replied.
X 14. Great!" yelled Harry. Let's play some tunes."
C 15. "I practice a lot," said Jayne proudly.

"This is exactly what I'm saying! You can tell by my quotation marks!"

48

Quotation Marks

Directions: Use quotation marks and commas to punctuate these sentences correctly.

"Remember: quotation marks are used to enclose a speaker's exact words."

1. "No," Ms. Elliot replied, "you may not go."
2. "Watch out!" yelled the coach.
3. "Please bring my coat," called Renee.
4. After thinking for a moment, Paul said, "I don't believe you."
5. Dad said, "Remember to be home by 9:00 P.M."
6. "Finish your projects," said the art instructor.
7. "Go back," instructed Mom, "and comb your hair."
8. "I won't be needing my winter coat anymore," replied Mei-ling.
9. He said, "How did you do that?"
10. I stood and said, "My name is Rosalita."
11. "No," said Misha, "I will not attend."
12. "Don't forget to put your name on your paper," said the teacher.
13. "Pay attention, class," said our history teacher.
14. As I came into the house, Mom called, "Dinner is almost ready!"
15. "Jake, come when I call you," said Mother.
16. "How was your trip to France, Mrs. Shaw?" asked Deborah.

49

Apostrophes

Use an **apostrophe** (') in a contraction to show that letters have been left out. A **contraction** is a shortened form of two words, usually a pronoun and a verb.

Add an **apostrophe** and **s** to form the **possessive** of singular nouns. **Plural possessives** are formed two ways. If the noun ends in **s**, simply add an apostrophe at the end of the word. If the noun does not end in **s**, add an apostrophe and **s**.

Examples:
Contraction: He can't button his sleeves.
Singular possessive: The boy's sleeves are too short.
Plural noun ending in s: The ladies' voices were pleasant.
Plural noun not ending in s: The children's song was long.

Directions: Use apostrophes to punctuate the sentences correctly. The first one has been done for you.

1. I can't understand that child's game.
2. The farmers' wagons were lined up in a row.
3. She didn't like the chairs' covers.
4. Our parents' beliefs are often our own.
5. Sandy's mother's aunt isn't going to visit.
6. Two ladies from work didn't show up.
7. The citizen's group wasn't very happy.
8. The colonists' demands weren't unreasonable.
9. The mothers' babies cried at the same time.
10. Our parent's generation enjoys music.

Use John's pencil!

I can't. The lead's broken.

Directions: Write two sentences of your own that include apostrophes.

11. _____
12. _____

Answers will vary.

50

Singular Possessives

Directions: Write the singular possessive form of each word. Then, add a noun to show possession. The first one has been done for you.

1. spider __spider's web__
2. clock __clock's__
3. car __car's__
4. book __book's__ (Nouns will vary.)
5. Mom __Mom's__
6. boat __boat's__
7. table __table's__
8. baby __baby's__
9. woman __woman's__
10. writer __writer's__
11. mouse __mouse's__
12. fan __fan's__
13. lamp __lamp's__
14. dog __dog's__
15. boy __boy's__
16. house __house's__

51

Plural Possessives

Directions: Write the plural possessive form of each word. Then add a noun to show possession. The first one has been done for you.

1. kid __kids' skates__
2. man __mens'__ (Nouns will vary.)
3. aunt __aunts'__
4. lion __lions'__
5. giraffe __giraffes'__
6. necklace __necklaces'__
7. mouse __mice's__
8. team __teams'__
9. clown __clowns'__
10. desk __desks'__
11. woman __women's__
12. worker __workers'__

Directions: Write three sentences of your own that include plural possessives.

13. _____
14. _____ Answers will vary. ____
15. _____

52

Contractions

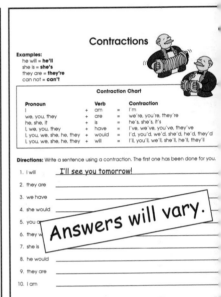

Examples:
he will = **he'll**
she is = **she's**
they are = **they're**
can not = **can't**

Contraction Chart

Pronoun		Verb		Contraction
I	+	am	=	I'm
we, you, they	+	are	=	we're, you're, they're
he, she, it	+	is	=	he's, she's, it's
I, we, you, they	+	have	=	I've, we've, you've, they've
I, you, she, he, they	+	would	=	I'd, you'd, we'd, she'd, he'd, they'd
I, you, we, she, he, they	+	will	=	I'll, you'll, we'll, she'll, he'll, they'll

Directions: Write a sentence using a contraction. The first one has been done for you.

1. I will __I'll see you tomorrow!__
2. they are _____
3. we have _____
4. she would _____
5. you a_____
6. they w____ Answers will vary.
7. she is _____
8. he would _____
9. they are _____
10. I am _____

53

Italics

Use **italics** or underlining for titles of books, newspapers, plays, magazines and movies.

Examples:
Book: Have you read *Gone with the Wind?*
Movie: Did you see *The Muppet Movie?*
Newspaper: I like to read *The New York Times.*
Magazine: Some children read *Sports Illustrated.*
Play: *A Doll's House* is a play by Henrik Ibsen.

Since we cannot write in italics, we underline words that should be in italics.

Directions: Underline the words that should be in italics. The first one has been done for you.

1. I read about a play titled Cats in The Cleveland Plain Dealer.
2. You can find The New York Times in most libraries.
3. Audrey Wood wrote Elbert's Bad Word.
4. Parents and Newsweek are both popular magazines.
5. The original Miracle on 34th Street was filmed long ago.
6. Cricket and Ranger Rick are magazines for children.
7. Bon Appetit means "good appetite" and is a cooking magazine.
8. Harper's, The New Yorker and Vanity Fair are magazines.
9. David Copperfield was written by Charles Dickens.
10. Harriet Beecher Stowe wrote Uncle Tom's Cabin.
11. Paul Newman was in a movie called The Sting.
12. Have you read Ramona the Pest by Beverly Cleary?
13. The Louisville Courier Journal is a Kentucky newspaper.
14. Teen and Boy's Life are magazines for young readers.
15. Have you seen Jimmy Stewart in It's a Wonderful Life?

54

Capitalization

Capitalize . . .
. . . the first word in a sentence
. . . the first letter of a person's name
. . . proper nouns, like the names of planets, oceans and mountain ranges
. . . titles when used with a person's name, even if abbreviated (Dr., Mr., Lt.)
. . . days of the week and months of the year
. . . cities, states and countries

Directions: Write **C** in the blank if the word or phrase is capitalized correctly. Rewrite the word or phrase if it is incorrect.

1. __C__ President Abraham Lincoln _____
2. __C__ Larry D. Walters _____
3. ____ saturn __Saturn__
4. ____ benjamin franklin __Benjamin Franklin__
5. __C__ August _____
6. __C__ professional _____
7. ____ jupiter __Jupiter__
8. __C__ Pacific Ocean _____
9. ____ white house __White House__
10. __C__ pet _____
11. __C__ Congress _____
12. __C__ Houston _____
13. __C__ federal government _____
14. ____ dr. Samuel White __Dr. Samuel White__
15. ____ milwaukee, Wisconsin __Milwaukee, Wisconsin__
16. ____ Appalachian mountains __Appalachian Mountains__
17. ____ lake michigan __Lake Michigan__
18. __C__ Notre Dame College _____
19. ____ department of the Interior __Department of the Interior__
20. ____ monday and Tuesday __Monday and Tuesday__

55

Review

Directions: Write a sentence using each type of punctuation correctly.

1. Semicolon _____
2. Colon _____
3. Apostrophe in a contraction _____
4. Comma _____
5. Quotation r____ Answers will vary.
6. Apostrophe (singular possessive) _____
7. Apostrophe (plural possessive) _____
8. Italics _____

Directions: Rewrite this sentence using correct capitalization and punctuation.

9. well said lisa its about time you came back from florida i expected you last tuesday

__"Well," said Lisa, "It's about time you came back from__
__Florida. I expected you last Tuesday."__

56

Review

Directions: Use semicolons to punctuate these sentences correctly.

1. I said yes; she said no.
2. He liked her; she felt differently.
3. It's hard to say; I don't know why.

Directions: Use colons to punctuate these sentences correctly.

4. At 10:45 P.M. the baby was still awake.
5. The article is in *Weekly Reader* 13:41.
6. Please order these: paper, pencils, pens and chalk.

Directions: Use dashes to punctuate these sentences correctly.

7. We all—especially Frank—felt overjoyed.
8. No one—least of all me—expected the surprise.
9. Our grandmothers—both of them—opened their gifts.

Directions: Use commas to punctuate these sentences correctly.

10. Yes, I'll put your name on the list.
11. Jessica, their youngest daughter, was beautiful.
12. He wanted catsup, tomatoes and lettuce on his burger.

Directions: Use quotation marks to punctuate these sentences correctly.

13. "I'll go!" shouted Matthew. "I like errands."
14. "Will you please," snarled her brother, "just be quiet!"

Directions: Use apostrophes to punctuate these sentences correctly.

15. The ladies' bonnets weren't very colorful.
16. Our children's names are special to us.

Directions: Underline the words that should be in italics.

17. Her favorite movie was The Wizard of Oz.
18. Have you read Sixes and Sevens by O. Henry?

57

Root Words

A **root word** is the common stem that gives related words their basic meanings.

Example: Separate is the root word for **separately, separation, inseparable** and **separator.**

Directions: Identify the root word in each group of words. Look up the meaning of the root word in the dictionary and write its definition. The first one has been done for you.

1. colorless, colorful, discolor, coloration
   Root word: _____color_____
   Definition: __any coloring matter, dye,__ __pigment or paint__

2. creator, creation, creating, creative, recreate
   Root word: __create__
   Definition: __to bring into being__

3. remove, movement, movable, immovable, removable
   Root word: __move__
   Definition: __to change the place or position of__

4. contentment, malcontent, discontent, discontentment
   Root word: __content__
   Definition: __happy with what one has__

5. pleasure, displeasure, pleasing, pleasant, unpleasant
   Root word: __please__
   Definition: __to be agreeable to__

6. successor, unsuccessful, successful
   Root word: __success__
   Definition: __a favorable outcome__

58

Suffixes

A **suffix** is a syllable added to the end of a root word that changes its meaning.

When a word ends in silent **e**, keep the **e** before adding a suffix beginning with a consonant.

Example: amuse + ment = amusement

Exception: argue + ment = argument

When a word ends in silent **e,** drop the **e** before adding a suffix beginning with a vowel.

Example: amuse = amusing

Exceptions: hoeing, shoeing, canoeing

Directions: Write **C** on the blank if the word in bold is spelled correctly. Draw an **X** in the blank if it is spelled incorrectly. The first one has been done for you.

_C_ 1. She was a woman of many **achievements.**
_C_ 2. He hated to hear their **arguments.**
_X_ 3. Do you want to go **canoing**?
_X_ 4. He kept **urgeing** her to eat more dessert.
_C_ 5. She was not good at **deceiving** others.
_C_ 6. He **rarely** skipped lunch.
_X_ 7. Would you repeat that **announcment**?
_C_ 8. Bicycle **safety** was very important to him.
_X_ 9. Their constant **argueing** got on my nerves.
_C_ 10. He found that **shoeing** horses was not easy.
_C_ 11. The sun felt hot as they were **hoeing.**
_X_ 12. She was so **relieveed** that she laughed.

59

Suffixes: Words Ending in Y

If a word ends in a vowel and **y**, keep the **y** when you add a suffix.

Example:
bray + ed = brayed
bray + ing = braying

Exception: lay + ed = laid

If a word ends in a consonant and **y,** change the **y** to **i** when you add a suffix unless the suffix begins with **i.**

Example:
baby + ed = babied
baby + ing = babying

Directions: Write **C** in the blank if the word in bold is spelled correctly. Draw an **X** if it is spelled incorrectly. The first one has been done for you.

_C_ 1. She was a good student who did well at her **studies.**
_X_ 2. Will you please stop **babing** him?
_X_ 3. She **layed** her purse on the couch.
_X_ 4. Both the **ferrys** left on schedule.
_C_ 5. Could you repeat what he was **saying**?
_X_ 6. He was **tring** to do his best.
_C_ 7. How many **cherries** are in this pie?
_C_ 8. The cat **stayed** away for two weeks.
_X_ 9. He is **saveing** all his money.
_C_ 10. The lake was **muddier** than I remembered.
_X_ 11. It was the **muddyest** lake I've ever seen!
_C_ 12. Her mother **babied** him when she was sick.

60

Suffixes: Doubling Final Consonants

If a one-syllable word ends in one vowel and consonant, double the last consonant when you add a suffix that begins with a vowel.

Examples: swim + ing = swimming   big + er = bigger

Directions: Add the suffixes shown to the root words, doubling the final consonants when appropriate. The first one has been done for you.

1. brim	+ ing	=	brimming
2. big	+ est	=	biggest
3. hop	+ ing	=	hopping
4. swim	+ er	=	swimmer
5. thin	+ er	=	thinner
6. spin	+ ing	=	spinning
7. smack	+ ing	=	smacking
8. sink	+ ing	=	sinking
9. win	+ er	=	winner
10. thin	+ est	=	thinnest
11. slim	+ er	=	slimmer
12. slim	+ ing	=	slimming
13. thread	+ ing	=	threading
14. thread	+ er	=	threader
15. win	+ ing	=	winning
16. sing	+ ing	=	singing
17. stop	+ ing	=	stopping
18. thrill	+ ing	=	thrilling
19. drop	+ ed	=	dropped
20. mop	+ ing	=	mopping

61

Suffixes: Doubling Final Consonants

When two-syllable words have the accent on the second syllable and end in a consonant preceded by a vowel, double the final consonant to add a suffix that begins with a vowel.

Examples: occur + ing = occurring   occur + ed = occurred

If the accent shifts to the first syllable when the suffix is added to the two-syllable root word, the final consonant is not doubled.

Example: refer + ence = reference

Directions: Say the words listed to hear where the accent falls when the suffix is added. Then add the suffix to the root word, doubling the final consonant when appropriate. The first one has been done for you.

1. excel	+ ence	=	excellence
2. infer	+ ing	=	inferring
3. regret	+ able	=	regrettable
4. control	+ able	=	controllable
5. submit	+ ing	=	submitting
6. confer	+ ing	=	conferring
7. refer	+ al	=	referral
8. differ	+ ing	=	differing
9. compel	+ ing	=	compelling
10. commit	+ ed	=	committed
11. regret	+ ing	=	regretting
12. depend	+ able	=	dependable
13. upset	+ ing	=	upsetting
14. propel	+ ing	=	propelling
15. repel	+ ed	=	repelled
16. prefer	+ ing	=	preferring
17. prefer	+ ence	=	preference
18. differ	+ ence	=	difference
19. refer	+ ing	=	referring
20. control	+ ing	=	controlling

EXCEL + ENCE = EXCELLENCE

62

117

Spelling: I Before E, Except After C

Use an **i** before **e**, except after **c** or when **e** and **i** together sound like long **a**.

Examples:
relieve
deceive
neighbor

Exceptions: weird, foreign, height, seize

i before e, except after c, or when sounding like a, as in "neighbor" and "weigh"

Directions: Write **C** in the blank if the word in bold is spelled correctly. Draw an **X** in the blank if it is spelled incorrectly. The first one has been done for you.

C 1. They stopped at the crossing for the **freight** train.
X 2. How much does that **wiegh**?
C 3. Did you **believe** his story?
X 4. He **recieved** an A on his paper!
X 5. She said it was the **nieghborly** thing to do.
C 6. The guards **seized** the package.
X 7. That movie was **wierd**!
X 8. Her **hieght** is five feet, six inches.
C 9. It's not right to **deceive** others.
X 10. Your answers should be **breif**.
C 11. She felt a lot of **grief** when her dog died.
X 12. He is still **greiving** about his loss.
C 13. Did the police catch the **thief**?
X 14. She was their **cheif** source of information.
C 15. Can you speak a **foreign** language?

63

Spelling: The Letter Q

In English words, the letter **q** is always followed by the letter **u**.

Examples:
question
square
quick

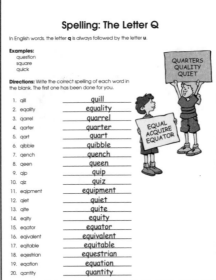

Directions: Write the correct spelling of each word in the blank. The first one has been done for you.

1. qill — quill
2. eqality — equality
3. qarrel — quarrel
4. qarter — quarter
5. qart — quart
6. qibble — quibble
7. qench — quench
8. qeen — queen
9. qip — quip
10. qiz — quiz
11. eqipment — equipment
12. qiet — quiet
13. qite — quite
14. eqity — equity
15. eqator — equator
16. eqivalent — equivalent
17. eqitable — equitable
18. eqestrian — equestrian
19. eqation — equation
20. qantity — quantity

64

Prefixes

A **prefix** is a syllable added to the beginning of a word that changes its meaning. The prefixes **in, il, ir** and **im** all mean **not**.

Directions: Create new words by adding **in, il, ir** or **im** to these root words. Use a dictionary to check that the new words are correct. The first one has been done for you.

	Prefix		Root Word		New Word
1.	il	+	logical	=	illogical
2.	il	+	literate	=	illiterate
3.	im	+	patient	=	impatient
4.	im	+	probable	=	improbable
5.	ir	+	reversible	=	irreversible
6.	ir	+	responsible	=	irresponsible
7.	in	+	active	=	inactive
8.	im	+	moral	=	immoral
9.	ir	+	removable	=	irremovable
10.	il	+	legible	=	illegible
11.	im	+	mature	=	immature
12.	im	+	perfect	=	imperfect

65

Prefixes

The prefixes **un** and **non** also mean **not**.

Examples:
Unhappy means not happy.
Nonproductive means not productive.

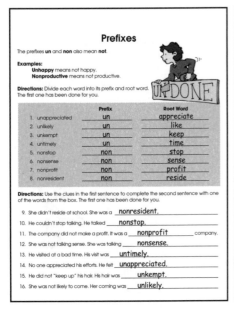

Directions: Divide each word into its prefix and root word. The first one has been done for you.

	Prefix	Root Word
1. unappreciated	un	appreciate
2. unlikely	un	like
3. unkempt	un	keep
4. untimely	un	time
5. nonstop	non	stop
6. nonsense	non	sense
7. nonprofit	non	profit
8. nonresident	non	reside

Directions: Use the clues in the first sentence to complete the second sentence with one of the words from the box. The first one has been done for you.

9. She didn't reside at school. She was a **nonresident.**
10. He couldn't stop talking. He talked **nonstop.**
11. The company did not make a profit. It was a **nonprofit** company.
12. She was not talking sense. She was talking **nonsense.**
13. He visited at a bad time. His visit was **untimely.**
14. No one appreciated his efforts. He felt **unappreciated.**
15. He did not "keep up" his hair. His hair was **unkempt.**
16. She was not likely to come. Her coming was **unlikely.**

66

Suffixes

The suffix **less** means **lacking** or **without**. The suffix **some** means **full** or **like**.

Examples:
Hopeless means without hope.
Awesome means filled with awe.

Directions: Create new words by adding **some** or **less** to these root words. Use a dictionary to check that the new words are correct. The first one has been done for you.

	Root Word		Suffix		New Word
1.	heart	+	less	=	heartless
2.	trouble	+	some	=	troublesome
3.	home	+	less	=	homeless
4.	humor	+	less	=	humorless
5.	awe	+	some	=	awesome
6.	child	+	less	=	childless
7.	win	+	some	=	winsome

Directions: Use the clues in the first sentence to complete the second sentence with one of the words from the box. The first one has been done for you.

8. Her smile was winning and delightful. She had a **winsome** smile.
9. The mean man seemed to have no heart. He was **heartless.**
10. She never smiled or laughed. She appeared to be **humorless.**
11. The solar system fills me with awe. It is **awesome.**
12. The couple had no children. They were **childless.**
13. He had no place to live. He was **homeless.**
14. The pet caused the family trouble. It was **troublesome.**

67

Suffixes

The suffix **ment** means the **act of** or **state of**. The suffixes **ible** and **able** mean **able to**.

Directions: Create new words by adding **ment** or **able** to these root words. Use a dictionary to check that the new words are correct. The first one has been done for you.

	Root Word		Suffix		New Word
1.	rely	+	able	=	reliable
2.	retire	+	ment	=	retirement
3.	sense	+	ible	=	sensible
4.	commit	+	ment	=	commitment
5.	repair	+	able	=	repairable
6.	love	+	able	=	loveable (also lovable)
7.	quote	+	able	=	quotable
8.	honor	+	able	=	honorable

Directions: Use the clues in the first sentence to complete the second sentence with one of the words from the box. The first one has been done for you.

9. Everyone loved her. She was **loveable (also lovable).**
10. He had a lot of sense. He was **sensible.**
11. She committed time to the project. She made a **commitment.**
12. He always did the right thing. His behavior was **honorable.**
13. The tire could not be fixed. It was not **repairable.**
14. They would not buy the car. The car was not **reliable.**
15. He gave the reporter good comments. His comments were **quotable.**
16. She was ready to retire. She looked forward to **retirement.**

68

Synonyms

Synonyms are words that have the same or almost the same meaning.

Examples:
small and **little**
big and **large**
bright and **shiny**
unhappy and **sad**

SMALL! LITTLE!

Directions: Circle the two words in each sentence that are synonyms. The first one has been done for you.

The (small) girl petted the (little) kitten.

I gave him a (present) and she brought a (gift) too.

She had a (pretty) smile and wore a (beautiful) sweater.

The (huge) man had (enormous) muscles.

They were not (late) but we were (tardy).

I saw a (circular) window with (rounded) glass.

Her eyes (silently) asked us to be (quiet).

The dog was (cowardly); she was really (afraid) of everything.

He wasn't (rich), but everyone said he was (wealthy).

Did you see the (filthy) cat with the (dirty) fur?

She's very (intelligent)—and her brother is (smart) too.

He (jumped) over the puddle and (leaped) into the air.

The firefighters came (quickly) but the fire was already burning (rapidly).

She said the (baby) was cute and smiled at the (infant).

He threw a (rock) and she kicked at a (stone).

69

Antonyms

Antonyms are words that have opposite meanings.

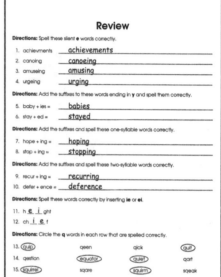
WE ARE ANTONYMS!

Examples:
big and **little**
pretty and **ugly**
common and **uncommon**
short and **tall**

awful	broad	cooked	inactive	dull
enemy	happy	smooth	stale	tardy
tiny	war	whisper	wonderful	wrong

Directions: Using words from the box, write the correct antonyms for the words in bold. The first one has been done for you.

1. It was hard to walk on the **narrow** streets. _broad_
2. He was an **enormous** person. _tiny_
3. Her answer was **correct**. _wrong_
4. The boy said he was **despondent**. _happy_
5. The fabric felt **rough** to her touch. _smooth_
6. His sense of humor was very **sharp**. _dull_
7. The soup tasted **awful**. _wonderful_
8. She always ate **raw** carrots. _cooked_
9. He insisted the bread was **fresh**. _stale_
10. His singing voice was **wonderful**. _awful_
11. She was always **on time**. _tardy_
12. The butterfly was **lively**. _dull_
13. His **shout** was unintentional. _whisper_
14. He is my **friend**. _enemy_
15. "This is a time of **peace**," the statesman said. _war_

70

Review

Directions: Spell these silent **e** words correctly.

1. achievments _achievements_
2. canoing _canoeing_
3. amuseing _amusing_
4. urgeing _urging_

Directions: Add the suffixes to these words ending in **y** and spell them correctly.

5. baby + ies = _babies_
6. stay + ed = _stayed_

Directions: Add the suffixes and spell these one-syllable words correctly.

7. hope + ing = _hoping_
8. stop + ing = _stopping_

Directions: Add the suffixes and spell these two-syllable words correctly.

9. recur + ing = _recurring_
10. defer + ence = _deference_

Directions: Spell these words correctly by inserting **ie** or **ei**.

11. h _e_ _i_ ght
12. ch _i_ _e_ f

Directions: Circle the **q** words in each row that are spelled correctly.

13. (quip) qeen qick (quit)
14. qestion (equator) (quiet) qart
15. (squirrel) sqare (squirm) sqeak

71

Review

Directions: Use these words with prefixes and suffixes in sentences of your own.

prepackaged _____

underground _____

fixable _____

excitement _____

restless _____

Answers will vary.

Directions: Write three sets of antonyms.

_____
_____
_____

Directions: Write three sets of synonyms.

_____
_____
_____

72

Review

Directions: Add the prefix **un** or **non** to these root words.

1. friendly _unfriendly_
2. sense _nonsense_
3. profit _nonprofit_
4. known _unknown_

Directions: Add the suffix **less**, **ment** or **some** to these root words.

5. awe _awesome_
6. word _wordless_
7. amaze _amazement_
8. harm _harmless_

Directions: Identify the root word in each group of words below. Write it in the blank.

9. responsive, responding, responsive _respond_
10. repetitive, repetition, repeatable _repeat_

Directions: Write synonyms for these words.

11. skinny _____
12. overweight _____
13. unhappy _____
14. rainy _____

Directions: Write *Answers will vary.*

15. hot _____
16. profit _____
17. sorrow _____
18. friend _____

73

"Affect" and "Effect"

Affect means to act upon or influence.

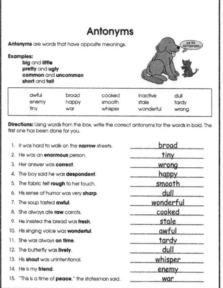
I HOPE ALL THIS STUDYING AFFECTS MY GRADE!

Example: Studying will **affect** my test grade.

Effect means to bring about a result or to accomplish something.

Example: The **effect** of her smile was immediate!

Directions: Write **affect** or **effect** in the blanks to complete these sentences correctly. The first one has been done for you.

affects 1. Your behavior (affects/effects) how others feel about you.
effect 2. His (affect/effect) on her was amazing.
effect 3. The (affect/effect) of his jacket was striking.
affect 4. What you say won't (affect/effect) me!
effect 5. There's a relationship between cause and (affect/effect).
effect 6. The (affect/effect) of her behavior was positive.
affected 7. The medicine (affected/effected) my stomach.
effect 8. What was the (affect/effect) of the punishment?
affect 9. Did his behavior (affect/effect) her performance?
affected 10. The cold (affected/effected) her breathing.
effect 11. The (affect/effect) was instantaneous!
affect 12. Your attitude will (affect/effect) your posture.
effect 13. The (affect/effect) on her posture was major.
effect 14. The (affect/effect) of the colored lights was calming.
affected 15. She (affected/effected) his behavior.

74

119

"Among" and "Between"

Among is a preposition that applies to more than two people or things.

Example: The group divided the cookies **among** themselves.

Between is a preposition that applies to only two people or things.

Example: The cookies were divided **between** Jeremy and Sara.

Directions: Write **between** or **among** in the blanks to complete these sentences correctly. The first one has been done for you.

between	1.	The secret is (between/among) you and Jon.
Between	2.	(Between/Among) the two of them, whom do you think is nicer?
among	3.	I must choose (between/among) the cookies, candy and pie.
among	4.	She threaded her way (between/among) the kids on the playground.
between	5.	She broke up a fight (between/among) Josh and Sean.
between	6.	"What's come (between/among) you two?" she asked.
between	7.	"I'm (between/among) a rock and a hard place," Josh responded.
among	8.	"He has to choose (between/among) all his friends," Sean added.
among	9.	"Are you (between/among) his closest friends?" she asked Sean.
between	10.	"It's (between/among) another boy and me," Sean replied.
among	11.	"Can't you settle it (between/among) the group?"
between	12.	"No," said Josh. "This is (between/among) Sean and me."
among	13.	"I'm not sure he's (between/among) my closest friends."
among	14.	Sean, Josh and Andy began to argue (between/among) themselves.
between	15.	I hope Josh won't have to choose (between/among) the two!

75

"All Together" and "Altogether"

All together is a phrase meaning everyone or everything in the same place.

Example: We put the eggs **all together** in the bowl.

Altogether is an adverb that means entirely, completely or in all.

Example: The teacher gave **altogether** too much homework.

Directions: Write **altogether** or **all together** in the blanks to complete these sentences correctly. The first one has been done for you.

altogether	1.	"You ate (altogether/all together) too much food."
all together	2.	The girls sat (altogether/all together) on the bus.
All together	3.	(Altogether/All together) now: one, two, three!
altogether	4.	I am (altogether/all together) out of ideas.
all together	5.	We are (altogether/all together) on this project.
altogether	6.	"You have on (altogether/all together) too much makeup!"
all together	7.	They were (altogether/all together) on the same team.
All together	8.	(Altogether/All together), we can help stop pollution (altogether/all together).
altogether	9.	He was not (altogether/all together) happy with his grades.
altogether	10.	The kids were (altogether/all together) too loud.
All together	11.	(Altogether/All together), the babies cried gustily.
all together	12.	She was not (altogether/all together) sure what to do.
all together	13.	Let's sing the song (altogether/all together).
altogether	14.	He was (altogether/all together) too pushy for her taste.
All together	15.	(Altogether/All together), the boys yelled the school cheer.

76

"Amount" and "Number"

Amount indicates quantity, bulk or mass.

Example: She carried a large **amount** of money in her purse.

Number indicates units.

Example: What **number** of people volunteered to work?

Directions: Write **amount** or **number** in the blanks to complete these sentences correctly. The first one has been done for you.

number	1.	She did not (amount/number) him among her closest friends.
amount	2.	What (amount/number) of ice cream should we order?
number	3.	The (amount/number) of cookies on her plate was three.
amount	4.	His excuses did not (amount/number) to much.
amounted	5.	Her contribution (amounted/numbered) to half the money raised.
number	6.	The (amount/number) of injured players rose every day.
amount	7.	What a huge (amount/number) of cereal!
number	8.	The (amount/number) of calories in the diet was low.
number	9.	I can't tell you the (amount/number) of friends she has!
amount	10.	The total (amount/number) of money raised was incredible!
number	11.	The (amount/number) of gadgets for sale was amazing.
number	12.	He was startled by the (amount/number) of people present.
amount	13.	He would not do it for any (amount/number) of money.
number	14.	She offered a great (amount/number) of reasons for her action.
number	15.	Can you guess the (amount/number) of beans in the jar?

77

"Irritate" and "Aggravate"

Irritate means to cause impatience, to provoke or annoy.

Example: His behavior **irritated** his father.

Aggravate means to make a condition worse.

Example: Her sunburn was **aggravated** by additional exposure to the sun.

Directions: Write **aggravate** or **irritate** in the blanks to complete these sentences correctly. The first one has been done for you.

aggravated	1.	The weeds (aggravated/irritated) his hay fever.
aggravated	2.	Scratching the bite (aggravated/irritated) his condition.
irritated	3.	Her father was (aggravated/irritated) about her low grade in math.
irritated	4.	It (aggravated/irritated) him when she switched TV channels.
irritated	5.	Are you (aggravated/irritated) when the cat screeches?
irritate	6.	Don't (aggravate/irritate) me like that again!
irritation	7.	He was in a state of (aggravation/irritation).
aggravates	8.	Picking at the scab (aggravates/irritates) a sore.
irritates	9.	Whistling (aggravates/irritates) the old grump.
irritated	10.	She was (aggravated/irritated) when she learned about it.
irritate	11.	"Please don't (aggravate/irritate) your mother," Dad warned.
aggravated	12.	His asthma was (aggravated/irritated) by too much stress.
aggravate	13.	Sneezing is sure to (aggravate/irritate) his allergies.
irritate	14.	Did you do that just to (aggravate/irritate) me?
irritated	15.	Her singing always (aggravated/irritated) her brother.

78

"Principal" and "Principle"

Principal means main, leader or chief, or a sum of money that earns interest.

Examples:
The high school **principal** earned interest on the **principal** in his savings account.
The **principal** reason for his savings account was to save for retirement.

Principle means a truth, law or a moral outlook that governs the way someone behaves.

Example:
Einstein discovered some fundamental **principles** of science.
Stealing is against her **principles**.

Directions: Write **principle** or **principal** in the blanks to complete these sentences correctly. The first one has been done for you.

principle	1.	A (principle/principal) of biology is "the survival of the fittest."
principles	2.	She was a person of strong (principles/principals).
principals	3.	The (principles/principals) sat together at the district conference.
principal	4.	How much of the total in my savings account is (principle/principal)?
principal	5.	His hay fever was the (principle/principal) reason for his sneezing.
principles	6.	It's not the facts that upset me. It's the (principles/principals) of the case.
principal	7.	The jury heard only the (principle/principal) facts.
principal	8.	Our school (principle/principal) is strict but fair.
principal	9.	Spend the interest, but don't touch the (principle/principal).
principle	10.	Helping others is a guiding (principle/principal) of the homeless shelter.
principle	11.	In (principle/principal), we agree; on the facts, we do not.
principal	12.	The (principle/principal) course at dinner was leg of lamb.
principles	13.	Some mathematical (principles/principals) are difficult to understand.
principal	14.	The baby was the (principle/principal) reason for his happiness.

79

"Good" and "Well"

Good is always an adjective. It is used to modify a noun or pronoun.

Examples:
We enjoyed the **good** food.
We had a **good** time yesterday.
It was **good** to see her again.

Well is used to modify verbs, to describe someone's health or to describe how someone is dressed.

Examples:
I feel **well**. He looked **well**.
He was **well**-dressed for the weather.
She sang **well**.

Directions: Write **good** or **well** in the blanks to complete these sentences correctly.

1. She performed ____well____.

2. You look ____good____ in that color.

3. These apples are ____good____.

4. He rides his bike ____well____.

5. She made a ____good____ attempt to win the race.

6. The man reported that all was ____well____ in the coal mine.

7. Jonas said, "I feel ____well____, thank you."

8. The team played ____well____.

9. Mom fixed a ____good____ dinner.

10. The teacher wrote, "____Good____ work!" on top of my paper.

80

"Like" and "As"

Like means something is similar, resembles something or describes how things are similar in manner.

Examples:
She could sing **like** an angel.
She looks **like** an angel, too!

As a conjunction, a joining word, that links two independent clauses in a sentence.

Example: He felt chilly **as** night fell.

Sometimes **as** precedes an independent clause.

Example: As I told you, I will not be at the party.

Directions: Write **like** or **as** in the blanks to complete these sentences correctly. The first one has been done for you.

_as_ 1. He did not behave (like/as) I expected.
like 2. She was (like/as) a sister to me.
like 3. The puppy acted (like/as) a baby!
_as_ 4. (Like/As) I was saying, he will be there at noon.
_as_ 5. The storm was 25 miles away, (like/as) he predicted.
like 6. He acted exactly (like/as) his father.
like 7. The song sounds (like/as) a hit to me!
like 8. Grandpa looked (like/as) a much younger man.
_as_ 9. (Like/As) I listened to the music, I grew sleepy.
_As_ 10. (Like/As) I expected, he showed up late.
like 11. She dances (like/as) a ballerina!
_as_ 12. (Like/As) she danced, the crowd applauded.
like 13. On stage, he looks (like/as) a professional!
_As_ 14. (Like/As) I thought, she has taken lessons for years.

81

Review

Directions: Use these words in sentences of your own.

1. affect _____
2. effect _____
3. among _____
4. between _____
5. irritate _____
6. aggravate _____
7. principal _____
8. principle _____
9. good _____
10. well _____
11. like _____
12. as _____

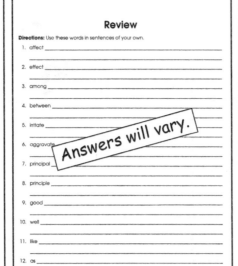

Answers will vary.

82

Review

Directions: Write the correct word in the blank.

effect 1. The (affect/effect) of the shot was immediate.
affected 2. The shot (affected/effected) her allergies.
effect 3. You have a positive (affect/effect) on me!
affected 4. I was deeply (affected/effected) by the speech.
between 5. The prize was shared (among/between) Art and Lisa.
among 6. She was (among/between) the best students in the class.
among 7. He felt he was (among/between) friends.
among 8. It was hard to choose (among/between) all the gifts.
irritate 9. Does it (irritate/aggravate) you to see people smoke?
aggravate 10. Does smoking (irritate/aggravate) his sore throat?
irritated 11. He wondered why she was (irritated/aggravated) at him.
irritation 12. The intensity of his (irritation/aggravation) grew each day.
principal 13. She had a (principal/principle) part in the play.
principal 14. Beans were the (principal/principle) food in his diet.
principles 15. She was a woman of strong (principals/principles).
principal 16. Mr. Larson was their favorite (principal/principle).
number 17. The (amount/number) of ice-cream cones he ate was incredible.
amount 18. I wouldn't part with it for any (amount/number) of money.
_as_ 19. It happened exactly (like/as) I had predicted!
like 20. He sounds almost (like/as) his parents.

83

Types of Analogies

An **analogy** shows similarities, or things in common, between a pair of words. The relationships between the words in analogies usually fall into these categories:

Purpose	One word in the pair shows the **purpose** of the other word (scissors: cut).
Antonyms	The words are **opposites** (light: dark).
Part/whole	One word in the pair is a **part**; the other is a **whole** (leg: body).
Action/object	One word in the pair involves an **action** with or to an **object** (fly: airplane).
Association	One word in the pair is what you think of or **associate** when you see the other (cow: milk).
Object/location	One word in the pair tells the **location** of where the other word, an **object**, is found (car: garage).
Cause/effect	One word in the pair tells the **cause**; the other word shows the **effect** (practice: improvement).
Synonyms	The words are **synonyms** (small: tiny).

Directions: Write the relationship between the words in each pair. The first two have been done for you.

cow: farm	object/location
toe: foot	part/whole
watch: TV	action/object
bank: money	association
happy: unhappy	antonyms
listen: radio	action/object
inning: ballgame	part/whole
knife: cut	action/object
safe: dangerous	antonyms
carrots: soup	part/whole

84

Writing Analogies

Once you have determined the relationship between the words in the first pair, the next step is to find a similar relationship between another pair of words.

Examples:
Scissors is to **cut** as **broom** is to **sweep.**
Black is to **white** as **up** is to **down.**

Scissors cut. Brooms sweep. The first analogy shows the **purpose** of scissors and brooms. In the second example, up and down are **antonyms**, as are black and white.

Directions: Choose the correct word to complete each analogy. The first one has been done for you.

1. **Sky** is to **blue** as **grass** is to
   A. earth   B. green   C. lawn   D. yard   _green_
2. **Snow** is to **winter** as **rain** is to
   A. umbrella   B. wet   C. slicker   D. spring   _spring_
3. **Sun** is to **day** as **moon** is to
   A. dark   B. night   C. stars   D. blackness   _night_
4. **5** is to **10** as **15** is to
   A. 50   B. 25   C. 30   D. 40   _30_
5. **Collie** is to **dog** as **Siamese** is to
   A. pet   B. kitten   C. baby   D. cat   _cat_
6. **Letter** is to **word** as **note** is to
   A. tuba   B. music   C. instruments   D. singer   _music_
7. **100** is to **10** as **1,000** is to
   A. 10   B. 200   C. 100   D. 10,000   _100_
8. **Back** is to **rear** as **pit** is to
   A. peach   B. hole   C. dark   D. punishment   _hole_

85

Analogies of Purpose

Directions: Choose the correct word to complete each analogy of purpose. The first one has been done for you.

1. **Knife** is to **cut** as **copy machine** is to
   A. duplicate   B. paper   C. copies   D. office   _duplicate_
2. **Bicycle** is to **ride** as **glass** is to
   A. dishes   B. dinner   C. drink   D. break   _drink_
3. **Hat** is to **cover** as **eraser** is to
   A. chalkboard   B. pencil   C. mistake   D. erase   _erase_
4. **Mystery** is to **clue** as **door** is to
   A. house   B. key   C. window   D. open   _key_
5. **Television** is to **see** as **CD** is to
   A. sound   B. hear   C. play   D. dance   _hear_
6. **Clock** is to **time** as **ruler** is to
   A. height   B. length   C. measure   D. inches   _measure_
7. **Fry** is to **pan** as **bake** is to
   A. cookies   B. dinner   C. oven   D. baker   _oven_
8. **Bowl** is to **fruit** as **wrapper** is to
   A. present   B. candy   C. paper   D. ribbon   _candy_

86

Antonym Analogies

Directions: Write antonyms for these words.

Answers will vary but may include:

1. run:	walk		15. awake:	asleep	
2. start:	stop		16. begin:	end	
3. laugh:	cry		17. increase:	decrease	
4. dependent:	independent		18. reverse:	forward	
5. young:	old		19. enlarge:	shrink	
6. North:	South		20. East:	West	
7. sink:	float		21. rural:	urban	
8. success:	failure		22. amateur:	professional	
9. combine:	separate		23. patient:	impatient	
10. laugh:	cry		24. rich:	poor	
11. polluted:	clean		25. empty:	full	
12. leader:	follower		26. fancy:	plain	
13. fascinate:	bore		27. introduction:	conclusion	
14. man:	woman		28. modern:	old-fashion	

Directions: Write two antonym analogies of your own.

29. _____

Answers will vary.

30. _____

87

Part/Whole Analogies

Directions: Determine whether each analogy is whole to part or part to whole by studying the relationship between the first pair of words. Then choose the correct word to complete each analogy. The first one has been done for you.

1. **Shoestring** is to **shoe** as **brim** is to
   A. cup   B. shade   C. hat   D. scarf   **hat**

2. **Egg** is to **yolk** as **suit** is to
   A. clothes   B. shoes   C. business   D. jacket   **jacket**

3. **Stanza** is to **poem** as **verse** is to
   A. rhyme   B. singing   C. song   D. music   **song**

4. **Wave** is to **ocean** as **branch** is to
   A. stream   B. lawn   C. office   D. tree   **tree**

5. **Chicken** is to **farm** as **giraffe** is to
   A. animal   B. zoo   C. tall   D. stripes   **zoo**

6. **Finger** is to **nail** as **leg** is to
   A. arm   B. torso   C. knee   D. walk   **knee**

7. **Player** is to **team** as **inch** is to
   A. worm   B. measure   C. foot   D. short   **foot**

8. **Peak** is to **mountain** as **crest** is to
   A. wave   B. ocean   C. beach   D. water   **wave**

88

Action/Object Analogies

Directions: Determine whether each analogy is action/object or object/action by studying the relationship between the first pair of words. Then choose the correct word to complete each analogy. The first one has been done for you.

1. **Mow** is to **grass** as **shear** is to
   A. cut   B. fleece   C. sheep   D. barber   **sheep**

2. **Rod** is to **fishing** as **gun** is to
   A. police   B. crime   C. shoot   D. hunting   **hunting**

3. **Ship** is to **captain** as **airplane** is to
   A. fly   B. airport   C. pilot   D. passenger   **pilot**

4. **Car** is to **mechanic** as **body** is to
   A. patient   B. doctor   C. torso   D. hospital   **doctor**

5. **Cheat** is to **exam** as **swindle** is to
   A. criminal   B. business   C. crook   D. crime   **business**

6. **Actor** is to **stage** as **surgeon** is to
   A. patient   B. hospital   C. operating room   D. knife   **operating roo**

7. **Ball** is to **throw** as **knife** is to
   A. cut   B. spoon   C. dinner   D. silverware   **cut**

8. **Lawyer** is to **trial** as **surgeon** is to
   A. patient   B. hospital   C. operation   D. operating room   **operatior**

89

Analogies of Association

Directions: Choose the correct word to complete each analogy. The first one has been done for you.

1. **Flowers** are to **spring** as **leaves** are to
   A. rakes   B. trees   C. fall   D. green   **fall**

2. **Ham** is to **eggs** as **butter** is to
   A. fat   B. toast   C. breakfast   D. spread   **toast**

3. **Bat** is to **swing** as **ball** is to
   A. throw   B. dance   C. base   D. soft   **throw**

4. **Chicken** is to **egg** as **cow** is to
   A. barn   B. calf   C. milk   D. beef   **milk**

5. **Bed** is to **sleep** as **chair** is to
   A. sit   B. couch   C. relax   D. table   **sit**

6. **Cube** is to **square** as **sphere** is to
   A. circle   B. triangle   C. hemisphere   D. spear   **circle**

7. **Kindness** is to **friend** as **cruelty** is to
   A. meanness   B. enemy   C. war   D. unkindness   **enemy**

8. **Pumpkin** is to **pie** as **chocolate** is to
   A. cake   B. dark   C. taste   D. dessert   **cake**

90

Object/Location Analogies

Directions: Write a location word for each object.

Answers will vary but may include:

1. shirt:	closet		15. dress:	dress shop	
2. milk:	carton		16. ice cream:	freezer	
3. vase:	table		17. table:	dining room	
4. screwdriver:	toolbox		18. medicine:	pharmacy	
5. cow:	barn		19. dog:	doghouse	
6. chalkboard:	classroom		20. basketball:	hoop	
7. shower:	bathroom		21. bed:	bedroom	
8. cucumbers:	garden		22. roses:	vase	
9. silverware:	drawer		23. dishwasher:	kitchen	
10. car:	garage		24. toys:	toy box	
11. pages:	book		25. cookies:	cookie jar	
12. bees:	beehive		26. bird:	birdhouse	
13. money:	bank		27. seashells:	beach	
14. salt water:	sea		28. asteroids:	sky	

91

Cause/Effect Analogies

Directions: Determine whether the analogy is cause/effect or effect/cause by studying the relationship between the first pair of words. Then choose the correct word to complete each analogy. The first one has been done for you.

1. **Ashes** are to **flame** as **darkness** is to
   A. light   B. daylight   C. eclipse   D. sun   **eclipse**

2. **Strong** is to **exercising** as **elected** is to
   A. office   B. senator   C. politician   D. campaigning   **campaigni**

3. **Fall** is to **pain** as **disobedience** is to
   A. punishment   B. morals   C. behavior   D. carelessness   **punishmer**

4. **Crying** is to **sorrow** as **smiling** is to
   A. teeth   B. mouth   C. joy   D. friends   **joy**

5. **Germ** is to **disease** as **war** is to
   A. soldiers   B. enemies   C. destruction   D. tanks   **destructic**

6. **Distracting** is to **noise** as **soothing** is to
   A. balm   B. warmth   C. hugs   D. music   **music**

7. **Food** is to **nutrition** as **light** is to
   A. vision   B. darkness   C. sunshine   D. bulb   **vision**

8. **Clouds** are to **rain** as **winds** are to
   A. springtime   B. hurricanes   C. clouds   D. March   **hurrican**

92

Synonym Analogies

Directions: Write synonyms for these words.

Answers will vary but may include:

1. miniature: _tiny_
2. wind: _gale_
3. picture: _photo_
4. quiet: _silent_
5. run: _jog_
6. cloth: _material_
7. mean: _nasty_
8. cup: _mug_
9. sweet: _tasty_
10. difficult: _hard_
11. obey: _do_
12. plenty: _lots_
13. scent: _smell_
14. sudden: _quick_

15. gigantic: _huge_
16. rain: _shower_
17. cabinet: _cupboard_
18. loud: _noisy_
19. leap: _jump_
20. jeans: _pants_
21. kind: _nice_
22. dish: _plate_
23. feline: _cat_
24. simple: _easy_
25. beautiful: _pretty_
26. scorch: _burn_
27. story: _tale_
28. thaw: _unfreeze_

Directions: Write two synonym analogies of your own.

Answers will vary.

93

Review

Directions: Name the type of analogy represented by each pair of words.

1. spoon: stir _object/action or purpose_
2. above: beneath _antomyms_
3. Thanksgiving: turkey _association_
4. flour: cookies _part/whole_
5. pollen: sneeze _cause/effect_
6. horse: barn _object/location_

Directions: Choose the correct word to complete each analogy.

1. **Paint** is to **artist** as **clay** is to
   A. pots   B. dirt   C. bricks   D. potter   _potter_

2. **Mumble** is to **talk** as **scrawl** is to
   A. paper   B. pen   C. signature   D. write   _write_

3. **Whisper** is to **quiet** as **screech** is to
   A. disturbing   B. silent   C. loud   D. shriek   _loud_

4. **Land** is to **sea** as **dry** is to
   A. paper   B. wet   C. sand   D. eyes   _wet_

94

Similes

A **simile** compares two things that are not alike. The words **like** or **as** are used to make the comparison.

Examples:
Her eyes sparkled **like** stars.
He was as kind **as** a saint.

Directions: Complete the similes. The first one has been done for you.

1. Mason was as angry as _a snapping turtle._
2. His smile was like _____
3. The baby cried like _____
4. I am as happy as _____
5. The dog barked like _____
6. Her voice was like _____
7. The child _____
8. My heart f _____
9. The sunshine looked like _____
10. The river was as deep as _____
11. The black clouds looked like _____
12. Her words sounded like _____
13. My eyes flashed like _____
14. His smile was as bright as _____
15. The fog was like _____

Answers will vary.

95

Metaphors

A **metaphor** is a type of comparison that says one thing *is* another. Depending on the tense used, **was** and **are** may also be used in a metaphor. The words **like** or **as** are not used in a metaphor.

Examples:
The boy's skinny legs **are sticks**.
Her smile was a **ray of sunshine**.

Use nouns in your comparison. Do not use adverbs or adjectives. A metaphor says one thing *is* another. The other thing must also be a noun. A metaphor is not literally true. That is why it is called a type of "figurative language."

Example:
Correct: The sunshine is a **blanket** of warmth. **Blanket** is a noun.
Incorrect: The sunshine is **warm**. **Warm** is an adjective.

Directions: Complete the metaphors. The first one has been done for you.

1. In the evening, the sun is a/an _big, bright penny._
2. At night, the moon is a/an _____
3. When you're sad, a friend is a/an _____
4. My mother is a/an _____
5. The doctor was a/an _____
6. The peaceful lake is a/an _____
7. Her pesky dog is a/an _____
8. His vivid ima _____
9. Our vaca _____
10. The twisting _____
11. The constantly buzzing fly is a/an _____
12. The smiling baby is a/an _____
13. His straight white teeth are a/an _____
14. The bright blue sky is a/an _____
15. The soft green grass is a/an _____

Answers will vary.

96

Poetry

Format:
Line 1: Name
Line 2: Name is a (metaphor)
Line 3: He/she is like (simile)
Line 4: He/she (three action words)
Line 5: He/she (relationship)
Line 6: Name

Example:
Jessica
Jessica is a joy.
She is like a playful puppy.
She tumbles, runs and laughs.
She's my baby sister!
Jessica

Directions: Build a poem that describes a friend or relative by using similes, metaphors and other words of your choice. Follow the form of the example poem.

Poems will vary.

97

Poetry: Haiku

Haiku is a type of unrhymed Japanese poetry with three lines. The first line has five syllables. The second line has seven syllables. The third line has five syllables.

Example:

Katie

Katie is my dog.
She likes to bark and chase balls.
Katie is my friend.

Directions: Write a haiku about a pet and another about a hobby you enjoy. Be sure to write a title on the first line.

Pet _____

_____

_____

_____

Hobby _____

_____

_____

_____

Poems will vary.

98

Poetry: Diamanté (99)

A **diamanté** is a poem in the shape of a diamond. Diamantés have seven lines with this format:

Line 1: one-word noun, opposite of word in line 7
Line 2: two adjectives describing line 1
Line 3: three **ing** or **ed** words about line 1
Line 4: two nouns about line 1 and two nouns about line 7
Line 5: three **ing** or **ed** words about line 7
Line 6: two adjectives describing line 7
Line 7: one word noun, opposite of word in line 1

Example:

child
happy, playful
running, singing, laughing
toys, games, job, family
working, driving, nurturing
responsible, busy
adult

Directions: Write a diamanté of your own.

Poems will vary.

99

Friendly Letters (100)

Directions: Study the format for writing a letter to a friend. Then answer the questions.

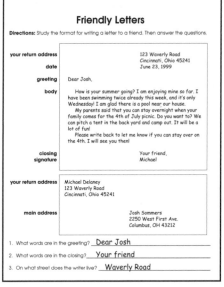

your return address — 123 Waverly Road / Cincinnati, Ohio 45241
date — June 23, 1999
greeting — Dear Josh,
body — How is your summer going? I am enjoying mine so far. I have been swimming twice already this week, and it's only Wednesday! I am glad there is a pool near our house.
My parents said that you can stay overnight when your family comes for the 4th of July picnic. Do you want to? We can pitch a tent in the back yard and camp out. It will be a lot of fun!
Please write back to let me know if you can stay over on the 4th. I will see you then!
closing / signature — Your friend, Michael

your return address — Michael Delaney / 123 Waverly Road / Cincinnati, Ohio 45241

main address — Josh Sommers / 2250 West First Ave. / Columbus, OH 43212

1. What words are in the greeting? **Dear Josh**
2. What words are in the closing? **Your friend**
3. On what street does the writer live? **Waverly Road**

100

Friendly Letters (101)

Directions: Follow the format for writing a letter to a friend. Don't forget to address the envelope!

Letters will vary.

101

Review (102)

Directions: Write **metaphor** or **simile** in the blanks.

1. She's an angel! — metaphor
2. He sings like a bird. — simile
3. My sister is a snake. — metaphor
4. The baby sleeps like a kitten. — simile

Directions: Label the parts of this friendly letter.

your return address — 2250 West First Ave. / Columbus, Ohio 43212
date — June 30, 1999
greeting — Dear Michael,
body — Sounds like you are having a great summer! I have been swimming, too, but not as often as you have! Maybe we can go swimming on the 4th after our families have the picnic. My mom and dad said I could stay over and camp with you. I will take the bus home the next afternoon. I will bring my sleeping bag and a lantern for us to use to scare off any bears, hah, hah.
See you next week!
closing / signature — Your friend, Josh
your return address — Josh Sommers / 2250 West First Ave. / Columbus, OH 43212
main address — Michael Delaney / 123 Waverly Road / Cincinnati, Ohio 45241

102

Cumulative Review (103)

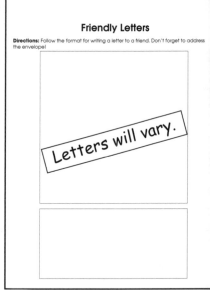

Directions: Identify the part of speech of the words in bold. The first one has been done for you.

1. The dog ran **across** the field. — preposition
2. My **parents** allow me to stay up until 10:00 P.M. — noun as subject
3. Our cat **is** long-haired. — verb
4. Matt will wash the **dirty** dishes. — adjective
5. Joseph washed the **car** on Saturday. — noun as direct object
6. The waterfall crashed **over** the cliff. — preposition
7. What will you give **her**? — personal pronoun
8. The car **rolled** to a stop. — verb
9. He **slowly** finished his homework. — adverb
10. My **nephew** will be 12 years old on Sunday. — noun as subject
11. The news program discussed the **war**. — noun as direct object
12. Our **family** portrait was taken in the gazebo. — adjective
13. I **would like** to learn to fly a plane. — verb
14. **My** hair needs to be trimmed. — possessive pronoun
15. **Strawberry** jam is her favorite. — adjective
16. The horse **quickly** galloped across the field. — adverb
17. **What** will you do next? — interrogative pronoun
18. Please stand **and** introduce yourself. — conjunctive
19. My neighbor takes **great** pride in her garden. — adjective
20. She sang **well** tonight. — adverb
21. My grandmother is from **Trinidad**. — noun as object of preposisiton

103

Cumulative Review (104)

Directions: Write sentences containing the items listed.

1. Appositive
2. Compound subject
3. Antecedent and pronoun
4. Correct use of the word **well**
5. Commas for words in a series
6. Direct add...
7. Compound...
8. Singular possessive
9. Plural possessive
10. Compound sentence
11. Correct use of quotation marks
12. Correct use of the word **effect**

Answers will vary.

104

Crossword Puzzle

Directions: Complete the crossword puzzle by using the clues.

ACROSS:

A _____ uses the words **like** or **as** to make a comparison.

_____ modify verbs.

An _____ tells to whom or for whom the action is performed.

The _____ of the sentence is the person, place, thing or idea the sentence is about.

Pairs of words which show relationships between words are called _____ .

Words that have opposite meanings are called _____ .

Words that have similar meanings are called _____ .

DOWN:

An _____ is a phrase which provides more information about a previous noun.

The _____ of the sentence is a verb that tells what the subject is doing.

A _____ answers what or whom after the verb.

Words that describe nouns are called _____

_____ compare two things by saying one is another.

_____ take the place of nouns.

105

Teaching Suggestions

Poetry

There are many different types of poetry besides haiku, diamanté and descriptive poetry. Try these poetry styles with your child.

Verb Poems: Many action words can be arranged on paper so the shape represen the action. Encourage your child to create his/her own action verb poems.

Example:

```
          ping        ping        ping        ping
    hop        hop        hop        hop        hop

        p
          o
            u
              r
                i
                  n
                    g
```

Limericks: Limericks are short, funny, five-line poems. The first, second and fifth lines rhyme. The second and third lines rhyme as well. Edward Lear (1812–1888) first popularized limericks. Read the example and other limericks out loud together.

Example:

There is a fat cat in my town
Whose fur is all spotted with brown;
He spends his days,
In a variety of ways,
Strolling in the park with a clown.

Have your child use this sentence as the first line and complete the limerick. Then have him/her complete one of his/her own.

There was an old horse from Bellaire

_____

_____

_____

_____

etaphor and Simile Poems: Have your child use metaphors and similes to create
s/her own poetry.

ample:	Metaphor	The clouds in the sky,
		Are popcorn rolling by.
	Simile	Elephants' noses
		Are like firemen's hoses.
		They squirt and they shower,
		With plenty of power.

ave your child illustrate the poems for greater visual effect.

anka: Tanka is an extension of haiku. Tankas complete the poet's thoughts by
dding two extra lines of seven syllables each at the end. Remember, haiku has
ree lines of five, seven and five syllables, respectively.

ample: Snow is falling down.
Crystals collect on the ground.
Winter has arrived.
Snowmen will soon decorate
The yards of children in town.

ave your child begin by composing a haiku. Then have him/her add two
dditional lines to make the poem a tanka.

hanging Prose to Poetry

)ften, colorful writing in essays, narratives, speeches and advertisements can
e easily transformed into poetry. Read the example with your child. Then look
or other topics and create your own poem together.

xample: HOUSE FOR SALE: This lovely home is situated on rolling ground in the
country. Horses frolic in the pasture by day, and retire to a well-kept barn at
ight. Lush forests surround the estate and offer plentiful wildlife along the
vinding paths.

'oem: I would love to live in a house,
Surrounded by nature and silence.
I would ride my horse through the woods,
And enjoy the sights and sounds of the forest.
I dream of being at peace,
Relaxed and care-free.
Alone in my beautiful house,
Surrounded by nature and silence.

Writing an Invitation

An invitation needs to include the time, date and place for an event, the reason for the invitation, and tell whether the receiver should indicate his/her ability to attend (RSVP). Invitations may be written in paragraph form, but it is often much easier to follow the example below.

You're Invited!

We're having a party for Mom and Dad's 50th Anniversary!
Date: September 10, 2001
Time: 5:00 P.M.–9:00 P.M.
Place: McFrange Party Center
RSVP: Mary at 555-1234 by September 1, 2001
Dinner will be served promptly at 5:30 P.M.
No gifts please.

Let your child create an invitation for your next birthday bash or other get-together. He/She can decorate the cards by hand, or use a computer to create an original card. Be sure to include all relevant information.

Writing a Thank You Note

Saying thank you in writing is a good habit for children to learn. Children should write thank you notes, not only for gifts, but also for thoughtful actions like an invitation from a friend's parents for dinner or an overnight visit. Help your child use proper form when composing a thank you note, even though it may be informal in nature or sent via e-mail. Read the example, and then have your child write a thank you note of his/her own.

December 28, 1999

Dear Grandma,

I received your package in the mail yesterday. I love the quilt you made for my new bedroom. It will match perfectly. I have decorated my room with wildlife, and your choice of the Canadian goose is perfect. Thank you for thinking of me.

Love,
Zach